The Competent Broker

The Competent Broker

Seeking Competence and Integrity
in the Real Estate Business

Reuben Moore

Copyright © 2020 by Reuben L. Moore

All rights reserved. No part of this publication may be reproduced or transmitted in any form or by any means, electronic or mechanical, including email and other digital transmission, written and other printed transmission, photocopy, recording, or inclusion in any information storage and retrieval system now known or to be invented, without permission in writing from the author, except by a reviewer who wishes to quote brief passages in connection with a review written for inclusion in a print or online publication, or online, cable, or over-the-air broadcast.

ISBN-13: 979-8650593386 (Paperback)

Edition: 20201014

Website
MooresRealEstate.blogspot.com

License Disclosure
The author of this publication, Reuben L. Moore, is an actively licensed North Carolina Real Estate Broker with the firm of Brick and Garden Real Estate in Cary, North Carolina. North Carolina Real Estate Commission License Number: 209969

Agency and Legal Disclaimer
Receipt of this publication, or reading this work, or any part of it, does not create an agency or fiduciary relationship of any kind between the author and any reader. Further, the author is not an attorney, and nothing in this publication should be construed as legal advice. If the reader needs legal advice, he or she should seek the services of a competent attorney.

Business and Financial Disclaimer
The author does not and cannot accept any responsibility for loss, financial or otherwise, by any individual or organization caused by acting on or refraining from action as a result of the material in this publication.

Cover photo: Edgar Bullon, Edgar Bullon Adventure Photography. (Licensed via Shutterstock)

Table of Contents

Introduction	1
Section One: Brokers	**5**
Chapter 1: The Two Primary Jobs of a Broker	6
Chapter 2: Sell Quickly and Get Paid Fast	8
Chapter 3: Underpricing	11
Buying the Listing	15
Chapter 4: Brokers Lack Business Savvy	16
Chapter 5: Brokers Lack Technical Skills	18
Chapter 6: Dual Agency and Broker Ethics	22
Chapter 7: Coming Soon	27
Chapter 8: Scripts & Objection Handling	30
Chapter 9: On Malarkey	35
Chapter 10: Licensing & Education	37
Chapter 11: Continuing Education and Ethics	39
Chapter 12: The REALTOR® Code of Ethics	41
Is there an Article 15 hearing in my future?	44
Chapter 13: Words to Watch: Coach & Team	49
Chapter 14: And Brokers Have Their Own Coaches	53
Chapter 15: Pushy Brokers are Stupid Brokers	58
Rhinestone Cowboys, Gunslingers & George Baileys	61
Section Two: Buyers & Sellers	**62**
Chapter 16: The Solid Brown Zebra	63
Chapter 17: The Pretense of Competence & Authority	65
Chapter 18: Ratings, Signaling, and Peer Reviews	68
Chapter 19: How to Find a Competent Broker	72

Chapter 20:	Anecdotal Advice	75
Chapter 21:	Objectivity	77
Chapter 22:	Real Estate Lags the Digital Age	81

Section Three: Fees & Business Models — 85

Chapter 23:	The Six Percent, Part One	86
Chapter 24:	The Discounters & Their Clients	89
Chapter 25:	Duty Shifting	92
Chapter 26:	On Paying Buyer's Brokers	96
Chapter 27:	A Coming Clash of Discounts	101
Chapter 28:	iBuyers	104
Chapter 29:	The Six Percent, Part Two	107
Chapter 30:	The Future Will Be Online	110
Chapter 31:	For Sale By Owner (FSBOs)	114

Section Four: Marketing — 120

Chapter 32:	Marketing is a Commodity	121
Chapter 33:	Marketing Will Not Sell Your House	127
	The Basics of Online Marketing	130
Chapter 34:	Open Houses are a Sham	136
Chapter 35:	Buyer Feedback	138
Chapter 36:	On Pricing Real Estate Like Groceries	142

Section Five: Negotiation — 146

Chapter 37:	The Negotiating Platform	147
Chapter 38:	Negotiating Due Diligence	152
	Negotiating Due Diligence: An Example	161
Chapter 39:	Try Not to Care (Too Much)	164
Chapter 40:	Be Deliberate	167

Chapter 41: On Seriousness	171
Chapter 42: Be Prepared	174
Chapter 43: On Cultural Differences	179
Chapter 44: Be Awake	182
Chapter 45: No Offer is Insulting	185
Chapter 46: Always Be Nice	189
The Andy Griffith Negotiation Strategy	192
Chapter 47: The Golden Rule	193
Chapter 48: Be Skeptical	195
Chapter 49: Excessive Talk & Clever Questions	198
Chapter 50: Discussion is Not Always Helpful	202
Chapter 51: Difficult People	205
Chapter 52: The No Response Response	209
Chapter 53: Watch Your Net, Not the Details	212
Chapter 54: Better Than Expected Offers	215
Chapter 55: On Win-Win	219
Conclusion: Gresham's Law for Real Estate	224
Afterword: Competence and Integrity	229
Glossary	232
Acknowledgements	*240*
About the author	*241*

Introduction

Competence is a choice.

This may be true in other fields as well, but in the business of real estate brokerage, this is an absolute. Further, I would argue that as fiduciaries, brokers have a duty to their clients to be competent. A *duty of competence*. How on earth can one act in the best interest of a client if one does not know how to achieve that best interest? Or worse, does not care enough to know? So competence is a character trait and a function of integrity.

It is not that brokers choose to be incompetent. Of course not. But they do choose to focus their attention elsewhere. Competence simply falls by the wayside. Unnoticed and unattended.

Now, a good number of readers will ask: Competence? What about excellence? Surely the goal is not mere competence, but rather *excellence* in all its glory? Two points on this. First, competence is a relative concept: Think *varying degrees of competence* or *he is the most competent surgeon I ever worked with*. For me personally, I think of the two terms almost interchangeably. And second, let's put this right here in the Introduction: Many and perhaps most brokers are not even merely competent in the minimal sense. Not by far. Let's focus on that before we bat around terms like *excellence*.

This book started as a sort of professional journal, a list of observations I made over the years. Call them truths, or rules, or just notes. Notes on brokers and how they conduct business, on buyers and sellers, on marketing and negotiation. Observations I have found useful and beneficial as a practicing broker.

But my notes are more than observations. Most come from my own less than ideal experiences: The unobserved and murky dynamics of the business, and the sometimes questionable incentives and motivations of those involved. So I crafted my notes to be aspirational, and they became goals. Goals for how I should conduct myself in this business.

They cover ethics and honesty and best practices. But mostly they are concerned with competence. How to be a competent broker. And what does competence look like in the business? It is not as obvious as one might think. So for me, these notes became a sort of *Code of Conduct*. Or even, a *Code of Competent Conduct*.

In the real estate business, competence and integrity are rare. Why is that? This is something I want to explore as we go through my notes. But I do have a theory: *The bad drives out the good*. Ponder that with me as we move forward, and we will come back to it in the Conclusion.

Now there is an unwritten rule in business that we should not criticize or say anything negative about our competitors. We all know this rule: *It is unprofessional to bad-mouth our competition*. It serves no purpose and only makes us look bad and small-minded. And let me assure you, I do tend to follow this rule in my business. There are exceptions, but basically, I give people my frank perspective, and they either love it or hate it. I rarely find the need to discuss how others conduct their business, good or bad.

But in a book subtitled, *Seeking Competence and Integrity in the Real Estate Business*, I think it is important to point out that our purpose here is not to create a good professional impression, nor is it to demonstrate proper business comportment. Rather, the purpose of this book is to help you find and identify competence and integrity in an often murky and counterintuitive business.

So yes, to that end, I will write disapprovingly of a great number of my fellow real estate brokers, and their firms, and the way they conduct themselves in this business. I may pay for this transgression later. But to do otherwise, there would simply be no point in writing this book. It would be a waste of my time and of the reader's time. And I assure you, I am not here to waste anyone's time.

Finally, for whom did I write this book? Who is my target audience? I think there are a few different and sometimes overlapping audiences.

First, people who are thinking about entering the real estate market either as buyers or sellers or both. First time buyers or sellers, yes absolutely. Or, perhaps you have had a less than ideal experience in the past. And now, you are seeking a better experience. Welcome.

A second audience is people thinking about getting a real estate license. Or perhaps you are a newly-minted broker, just finding your way. Yes, I would like to reach both of these groups. Hopefully you will read this work along side of more conventional material. And you can judge the probity of this work for yourself. You too are very welcome here.

Third, disaffected brokers, who with some experience, see the business for what it really is. Perhaps you are less than satisfied with the status quo and are seeking a better way. I hope you will find my perspective candid and refreshing. Yes, there is an alternative. Come, help me make a difference.

Section One:

Brokers

Chapter 1: The Two Primary Jobs of a Broker

Real estate brokers have two primary jobs: *Client Acquisition* and *Conveying Real Property*. These two jobs involve entirely different skill sets. In fact I would argue that the type of person who is good at either one of these jobs, that has the skill set to make them good at it, is almost always not the type of person who is good at the other. Many very successful brokers are quite brilliant at client acquisition, but not terribly competent at conveying real property.

~~~

To be successful in the real estate business, it is vital to have, or to generate, a stream of potential clients. In fact, this is so important that brokers will concentrate their time, effort, and money, on this aspect of the business to the detriment of all others. What you find is that the people who are most adept at this, do best in the business financially. And this does not go unnoticed by their colleagues.

As a consequence, transactional competence suffers industry-wide. Why become a better negotiator when you can make more money prospecting? In fact, why learn basic accounting, why keep up with contract and paperwork changes, the law, best practices, building techniques, technology, etc. The whole range of knowledge and experience and expertise that is useful and helpful for serving clients.

The most striking aspect of these two primary jobs is what they are not: *Salesperson*. Sure, many people believe that a real estate broker is a salesperson: *Brokers sell houses*. And many brokers continue to advance this misconception. But in today's real estate marketplace, this is almost entirely untrue.

Real estate is not a *sales* job. Not really. Rather, it is a *customer service* job. Whether a broker represents the buyer or the seller, in terms of the transaction, everything from first showing the house right through the closing, it is all customer service. No sales. Brokers do not sell houses; a house either meets the needs and desires of a buyer, or it does not. Even the basic marketing done by most brokers is more customer service than sales. We'll come back to this.

Now I don't want this to be about semantics. Some old-school salespeople will argue: Well look, sales is fifty percent customer service anyway. Okay fine. But if we are talking about real estate, it's more like ninety-nine percent. There's very little actual *house selling* in the real estate business. I know: It's heresy.

Now arguably, the client acquisition aspect of the job is a sales pursuit. But what is the product being sold? Well I can tell you this: It is not houses. No of course not; brokers are selling their service. They are selling the service of selling houses. This is a subtle but important distinction. Brokers pretend to sell houses in order to secure clients. Here, they are not *conveying real property,* rather they are *acquiring clients.*

The customer service aspect of the real estate business, the down and dirty, hands-on business of conveying real property requires transactional competence. I think it is fair to say that most brokers just do not have it.

Why? Because it is not important to them.

Chapter 2: Sell Quickly and Get Paid Fast

Brokers will gladly take the first acceptable offer or the offer that closes earliest. Why? Because this way they get paid faster. Brokers do not care about the highest and best offer for their client. They do not even care about which offer will pay them the highest commission. No, what they care about is getting paid as fast as possible.

So brokers will often take the first offer. Or perhaps an offer from an office colleague before the property even goes on the market. The broker will then brag about how quickly they got your property sold. But unless you specifically instructed your broker to dump the property as quickly as possible, ask yourself who wins and who loses in these situations?

~~~

My neighbors just sold their house. I am writing this in early 2020, a strong seller's market. With the advice of their broker, they put the house on the market on a Tuesday afternoon. And they had it under contract by early evening Friday, three days later. Now I am sure that they received multiple offers. But surely had they kept the house on the market through the weekend, they would have done better.

So why did they not?

Well sure, it could be that they said to their broker: *Look, this first offer is great, more than we expected, and all the showings are making us miserable; let's just take it and put a stop to all this hassle.* This does happen.

But you see these very quick sales far too often for this to be happening each and every time. And most people are not of that mindset. Most sellers want the best deal they can get.

And besides, two extra days? Just one weekend? Most sellers can tolerate that. Most people expect that. I mean, this is not going on for a month, much less six months.

And yet, many sellers will accept offers made on the first day or the first few days. Why?

Well their broker advises them to take it. *Look Mr. Seller, the first offer is usually the best offer and we certainly don't want to lose this buyer to another house. Let's get them locked down.*

Of course, in a strong seller's market, there aren't really any other houses!

But whether it is a seller's market or a buyer's market, and regardless of who the broker represents, the broker wants *a* deal more than he wants the *best* deal. Think of it like this: A $10,000 increase in the purchase price is at most $300 to the broker. No, no, let's get this wrapped up as soon as possible, so I get paid as soon as possible. I can live without another $300. And besides, I've got a nine o'clock tee time Saturday morning. And after that, I want to get back to prospecting.

But that attitude costs the seller ten thousand dollars.

On the buy side, it's even worse. Why should I fight to reduce the purchase price, when we can make a deal right now. And besides, if I do negotiate a lower price, heck, I get paid less.

When I first obtained my real estate license, I joined one of the large local brokerages here in our market. I was attending the regular Tuesday morning sales meeting. It may not have been my first meeting, but it was definitely in my first month there. One of the brokers stood up, described her new listing, as we all did, and then explained how she had already sold the house…in a mere eight hours. To cheers all around. They were literally jumping up and down, cheering.

I knew right then and there that I was in the wrong place.

The fact that she did not market this property to the entire potential buyer pool did not seem to bother her. The fact that she did not allow the entire interested buyer subset the possibility of viewing the property did not seem to bother her.

No, no, she put the house on the market, got an offer, and convinced her clients, the sellers, to take it. Objections be damned.

This is the height of irresponsibility: A complete lack of concern for her clients and an extreme disregard for her fiduciary duty to them.

And yet, she was so proud of it. And all the brokers in that room were so proud of her.

She went right out and had a new sign rider made:

Sold in Less than a Day!

Now, are there instances where a seller instructs his broker to dump the property as soon as possible no matter what? Of course there are. Think impending foreclosure. But these are the exceptions not the rule. And again, we see this behavior far too often for this to be a valid explanation.

No, the explanation is simple. The broker wants the property sold as quickly and as easily as possible. So she gets paid sooner, and with the least amount of time and effort.

To hell with the seller.

Chapter 3: Underpricing

For the same reason, brokers prefer to underprice properties. They will make all sorts of arguments about *pricing it right from the start* and not allowing the home to *become stale*. But I can think of no other product or asset class marketed this way. No, it is really about a quick sale and a quick payday.

~~~

Let's start this chapter with a conversation:

> **Broker:** So you can see Mr. & Mrs. Seller, the comparable properties indicate a sales price of $400,000-ish.
>
> **Seller:** Er, we were thinking of something more around $450,000.
>
> **Broker:** Hmm, tell me why?
>
> **Seller:** Well, for one thing, we've put about a fifty thousand dollars into the place since you sold it to us seven years ago
>
> **Broker:** Ah yes. Well, if you will remember, when you bought it, I cautioned you to be careful with upgrades and improvements. And to be sure you would enjoy them because you rarely get your money out of them.
>
> **Seller:** Oh yes, we remember, but that does not mean they are worth zero.

Broker: Well sure, we could go to $405,000 or stretch to $410,000. But it would really be just room for negotiation. If we were to start anywhere near $450,000 the house would just sit on the market and get stale.

Seller: Stale?

Broker: Yes, it is vital to *price a home correctly from the start*. So that it does not sit on the market too long and *become stale* and buyers will surely think: *There must be something wrong with that house*. Then, you'll end up taking even less than I am suggesting. Now, we don't want that, do we?

This conversation goes on everyday across the country. And I am here to tell you what no one else will: It is a sham.

As I mentioned above, can you think of any other product or asset class marketed this way? I can assure of this: The only reason a potential buyer might think that there is something wrong with the house is that their broker tells them so. Otherwise they would think the same thing they do when they go to buy anything else: It is natural and standard for sellers to start high and come down over time until the product sells.

Just think of when you go out to buy any other product. An article of clothing, a new or used car, furniture, etc. A real estate broker would have you believe that the brand new line of spring fashions should start at mid-summer pricing. It's crazy. And it is dishonest.

So sure, the seller's hoped-for price may be wishful thinking. But on the other hand, the seller may have very good reasons for their price: *This is a very popular neighborhood and there have been no sales in here for over a year. So Mr. Broker, your comparable properties are either older or from other neighborhoods. And we've talked to our neighbors; no one else is even thinking about selling.* Or the seller may say: *Well, we've got the time.*

So what's the alternative? Well, the conversation starts very similar to the above. But when the sellers say: Hey, we want $450,000, why not respond with:

> **Broker:** Okay, well it is really a question of price versus time. I have explained the comps to you; I believe that it will sell for around $400,000, but God knows I am not infallible. And your points about the neighborhood sales are well made. I tell you what, let's start at $450,000. And we can bring the price down on your schedule. Just don't be surprised if it does not sell until we come down substantially. And please, do not get frustrated with me for not *getting it sold* before then.

I mean, what does this cost the broker?

The answer is: A quick sale. And an easy sale.

And, the broker is worried that the seller will fire them for not *getting it sold*. But I think the broker needs to do two things. First, be honest about what he thinks the property is worth. And second, respect his seller. The seller's needs and desires are as important as the broker's. More important. Actually, the seller's needs should be paramount. Is it not sad that we must point this out?

I have found that if you begin the relationship this way, people will not fire you. They will remember what you said and think better of you for it.

This lack of respect for clients and potential clients is epidemic in the real estate business. We'll spend more time on this throughout this book.

But wait, I said it was a sham, right? For brokers, it is not only about getting the seller to accept less than they *want*. It is also about getting the seller to accept less than they *should*. The comparable properties typically indicate a price range, and the broker wants the seller at the bottom or even beneath that range. Again, quick sale, easy sale.

Plus, go back to my comment about price versus time. If you put the house on the market for three days, your buyer pool is, by definition, less than if you leave it on the market for, God-forbid, a whole week. And an expanded buyer pool increases the likelihood of an offer or of an acceptable offer, and surely of the best possible offer.

Now I hear you: No other brokers are telling us this. How come your advice is so much different? Remember *Freakonomics?* Economists found that when brokers sell their own properties, they price them higher and leave them on the market longer than when they sell client properties.[1] Why? Well if they are selling their own property, it's their money, not yours.

I am not saying there is absolutely no truth in this staleness business. I am just saying that brokers are being disingenuous about their goals.

After a broker lists a property, what does it cost the broker to leave it on the market for a few days or weeks? Nothing. Only bragging rights about a quick sale. And a quick payday.

---

[1] Steven Levitt & Stephen Dubner, *Freakonomics: A Rogue Economist Explores the Hidden Side of Everything*, William Morrow, 2005.

Buying the Listing

Many brokers will argue, if we follow your advice, we are seducing the sellers with an inflated and unrealistic price simply to secure the listing. They argue that this is just as dishonest as underpricing, because we know that we are overpricing the house and have every intent to lower the price in order to get the house sold (and get paid). They refer to this as *Buying the Listing*.

Well don't forget, I said above that brokers should be honest about what we think the house is worth. The difference really is a question of who, broker or seller, is in charge. I propose that we give the seller all of the information and let him make his own decisions. And yes, some sellers will rely on a broker's judgment more than others, or more quickly than others. That is perfectly okay. Again, respect your client.

But the worst part of the whole buying the listing argument is that it is self-serving. Because I hear this argument the most as a justification for underpricing. So if you hear it, hold on to your wallet.

Chapter 4: Brokers Lack Business Savvy

Residential real estate brokers are often not very business savvy. Many could benefit from some basic classes in accounting, interpersonal communications, negotiation, and yes, even marketing. And perhaps most importantly, on what it means to be a fiduciary.

~~~

I once sold a rental house that I owned. To begin with, I overpriced it. Of course I did. I left it on the market at that price for about a week. Then, I lowered the price one thousand dollars every day until it sold. After about a week of this, I think the price was down to around $224,000.

A broker calls me:

Broker: Will you take $210,000?

Me: Absolutely. In two weeks.

The broker was just baffled by this. It took her a moment, but then the conversation continued:

Broker: I don't understand. If you will take $210,000 in two weeks, why would you not take it today? (And I could tell, she was genuinely curious.)

Me: Because someone might just come along and buy it for more before then.

Broker: Well I've never heard of such. But okay, I'll call you back in two weeks.

But she did not call me back because I sold it for $218,000.

Now, I am not saying that this sales strategy is for everyone. Although I have always liked some version of this when a quick sale is needed without leaving a lot of money on the table. And the process can be halted at any point in favor of a negotiated price. But what is notable here is the complete lack of understanding of the broker.

Many brokers just don't have good business sense. And so they are not equipped to speak the language of business and negotiation. Instead, they speak the language of scripts and objection handling. In my example above, the broker was thrown because she simply did not have a script for that scenario. She really had never heard of such. We will come to scripts in Chapter Eight.

Look, brokers represent clients in a six-figure business transaction. Sometimes more. We simply must add value. This is a serious business. And brokers should approach this business with the thoughtful sobriety it deserves and attention it demands.

Now I mentioned above, what it means to be a fiduciary. But the truth is, I think most brokers know exactly what it means to be a fiduciary, *acting on behalf of another and putting that person's interests first and certainly ahead of your own*. I mean, the concept is not difficult. They just choose not to do so. Underpricing and quick sales are two examples we've used so far. There will be more as we continue. But notice how subtle these can be. This is intentional. Even if the principal noticed, it would be difficult to prove malfeasance on the part of the broker.

Oh, and that broker above: One of the most successful in my market.

Chapter 5: Brokers Lack Technical Skills

Further, many brokers are not terribly technologically savvy. This can be a mere inconvenience when engaging a broker. It can be a huge disadvantage in, say for example, a quick-moving multiple-offer scenario. Brokers do not need to be the most technically proficient people you deal with. But find a broker who is at least of average technological competence.

~~~

A broker calls late one Sunday morning. She had just shown one of our listings and she asked all the right questions. You can tell, serious buyer. At the end of the conversation, she says, okay, I'll send you an offer. Now in North Carolina, our standard form offer is fourteen pages. So it takes a while to put together. So later that day, I receive her email. With fourteen attachments. Fourteen jpeg attachments. Fourteen photo files. One for each page.

The offer itself was not bad at all. Full price, conventional financing, other terms okay. I spoke with the sellers who said, sure, send it over and we'll sign it. So the quickest thing I knew to do was to ask the broker to re-scan as one complete pdf document. She said that may take some time because her assistant was on vacation. So rather than wait, I started cropping her photos, converting each to a pdf, and then combining them. A time-consuming and imperfect solution, but it was doable.

About half way through this process, I get a call from another broker: Hey, did you get my email? Yes, you see where this is going. He had shown the house on Friday, and after viewing other houses on Saturday and Sunday morning, he had just emailed an offer. One thousand over list and all cash. So we go into multi-offer mode and the details of that are not important here. What is important is the sellers had been ready to sign the first offer. And after requesting best offers from both buyers and some negotiation, they ended up taking the second offer.

When I mentioned this to the first broker, she said: *Sweetie, I've been in this business 25 years and closed thousands of deals. What about you?* My response? *You're right, have a nice weekend.*

But one thing I can guarantee you: When she talked to her buyers, what do you think she told them? Simply: *We were outbid.* And how would they know otherwise?

Just think about this. Think about the trust that her buyers placed in her. And yet, they will never know just how misplaced that trust was.

Now I know what you're thinking: That must have been in 2008, or even earlier. No, this was late 2018.

Ah, the joy of working with real estate brokers.

While the digital revolution has transformed other industries, the real estate business remains stubbornly and notoriously anti-technology. Most brokers and firms simply do not value technology and what it can do for the business and their clients. Grudging modernization has come with extremely poor technology choices, not broker or client friendly, and certainly not cost-effective. This has been a consistent pattern over the last thirty years.

Many brokers are even proud of their lack of technical competence: *No sweetie, I don't need to learn your new technical thingie because my clients value my high-touch service*. Said, I assure you, with smug arrogance and condescension.

Nothing wrong with high-touch service. But it can be used as an excuse to keep prices high. And to not keep up-to-date. Keeping up-to-date takes time. I don't care how you learn. I know some people like to take classes. Some prefer structured self-taught programs. Some will watch Youtube videos. Some will actually read manuals. Me? I like to just play around with new software and gadgets. But however one does it, it does take time. Precious time away from *acquiring clients*.

Many brokers don't seem to understand that technology can add a level of convenience and service to the client. Or more likely, as with so many other aspects of the *conveying real property* side of the business, the brokers just don't care.

Technology is not important to them.

It is worth noting how many of these same brokers are all over social media. They spend oodles of time there and can easily detail the intricacies of each site. Why? Well, they view this as a *Client Acquisition* activity.

They may not be able to manipulate a pdf document. But they post to Facebook and Instagram multiple times a day, they serve as the *neighborhood lead* on Nextdoor, and judging by my inbox, they seem to believe that email marketing is a productive use of their time.

And if it is this bad for the obvious stuff, one can just imagine how bad it might be for the less obvious: A broker's back office technology or lack of technology. Document security and encryption, backup procedures, email security and wire fraud prevention, password management, financial records, etc. There is a lot of client data in a broker's hands. Does anyone really think that they give it the proper respect and attention it deserves.

Given the routine nature of pdf documents in the real estate business, is this not a valid indication of a broker's overall technological competence? Let me ask you this: If a broker cannot master pdf creation and manipulation, do you really think she has an adequate document security system in place?

I'm just asking.

Chapter 6: Dual Agency and Broker Ethics

Dual agency is bad for clients, both buyers and sellers. If you do not know what dual agency is, then you should educate yourself on this practice before you hire a broker. If a broker defends the idea of dual agency, you know immediately that they are not honest. Some brokers love dual agency because they get paid more, often double.

~~~

So the neighbor's dog escapes his fenced back yard and goes walk-about. He wanders into your yard, and while he's digging up your tulips, that tree, the dead one you've been meaning to cut down, falls on the dog. The dog may be injured or worse, but now we surely have some very upset neighbors. The first thing they say is: Hey, we were just talking last week about how dangerous that tree might be.

Right? You get it. This is America…so off we go to court.

Yep, right on cue, you get served. What to do? Well *who* knows *what* to do? That's why we have lawyers. So you ask around and hear great things about Attorney Fred. And you promptly schedule an appointment. You walk in and introduce yourself to Fred. And Fred asks: You're the Smith's neighbors? The one with the tree? Ah, er, yes. And Fred says, no problem, I will be delighted to represent you in this matter. But I need to inform you that the Smith's hired me last week to file suit against you for their injured canine.

No rational person would accept this. You'd thank Fred for his time, and go hire another attorney. In fact, this situation is a violation of the ethics of the bar, and would never be allowed.

Yet…yet in the real estate business, this happens every day across America. We even have a name for it: Dual Agency.

To discuss this further, I am going to borrow heavily from Bill Gassett's March 2019 article *Dual Agency Doesn't Benefit Consumers* which appeared on the REALTOR® Magazine website.[2]

Let me start by paraphrasing Gassett:

> To clarify, when I say dual agency, I'm referring to one broker representing *both* the buyer and the seller in a single transaction. In some states, dual agency can also mean two brokers working for the same firm, each representing one of the parties (often referred to as *designated agency*).

Now it is my belief that, with well thought out procedures, it is possible to responsibly practice designated agency. Though I should tell you, some scrupulously honest brokers do not agree. But in any case, it is my contention that single-agent dual agency is never responsible and never ethical. And should be illegal.

Gassett writes:

> First, you should know what it means to *represent* a client. You become his or her fiduciary, and

---

[2] Bill Gassett, REALTOR® Magazine: *Dual Agency Doesn't Benefit Consumers*, 26 March 2019. https://magazine.realtor/news-and-commentary/commentary/article/2019/03/dual-agency-doesn-t-benefit-consumers

All quotes in this chapter come from Bill Gassett's article and are used with his permission. Bill's article is definitely worth reading in full. Plus, I think the reader will find the comments to his article prove the point I am making here. Really, have a look.

everything you do should be in the client's best interests – even when it conflicts with your own. You are their confidant. This means counseling on price, negotiating in their best interests, advising on decisions such as home inspections, and the whole myriad of other things that come up in a sale. These are the normal duties of a real estate agent.

How do you, then, counsel a seller on setting the list price when you also must help the buyer get the best deal possible? Under dual agency situations, the real estate professional's interests collide head-on with their clients'. So, agents who practice dual agency either don't understand the gravity of this conflict – or they don't care.

Bill allows for the possibility that brokers do not understand the gravity of this conflict. Personally I am of the mind that they do understand it, but they just don't care. Gassett points out that states require brokers to explain to their clients exactly how dual agency works. Then he continues:

Here's the problem: The agent explaining dual agency has a vested interest in the client accepting it. [So] real estate agents who practice dual agency don't explain the downsides, including the fact that they may not be able to protect the client's best interests while also representing the other side. How do you think these agents will approach the [required] discussion with their clients? If the word *sugarcoat* comes to mind, you're right.

And why? Why do brokers act this way? Well, look at the broker's financial incentives. If the broker supposedly *represents* both sides, he gets paid on both sides. So as much as double.

Gassett concludes: *Practicing dual agency is a function of greed.*

The reader may be interested in a comment I posted to Bill's article:

> Explain dual agency to any other class of professionals, certainly attorneys, and then ask: Is this ethical? To others, the answer is obvious: No, that is unethical behavior. But if you put the question to a group of brokers, more than half will argue that it is ethical behavior. This is a problem.

And Bill responded:

> One of the worst parts of dual agency is the person explaining it has a vested interest in the client accepting it. Guess what that means – it isn't explained properly! What seller in sound body and mind would ever want someone they are paying thousands of dollars to, go from representing them to becoming a neutral party. How about zero!
> [emphasis removed]

Bill is quite rightly concerned about how dual agency is explained to clients. My concern is with the brokers themselves, who, I think, clearly understand the problems with dual agency. But who nevertheless practice this behavior anyway. And what this says about people in our business.

They are simply unethical.

I would like that to be the end of this chapter. But I think it fails to convey the scope of this problem. What the reader needs to understand is this: We are not talking about a few bad apples here. Dual agency is widely practiced. By how many brokers? If I had to guess, I'd say at least half, and probably quite a bit more. I am not sure if the financial incentives of the real estate business drive brokers to become unethical. Or, if unethical people are drawn to the business. Or both.

Finally as Bill Gassett points out at the end of his piece, it is worth noting that eight states have banned dual agency: Alaska, Colorado, Florida, Kansas, Maryland, Oklahoma, Texas, and Vermont. I wish this list was longer.

So, want to find an honest broker? Ask them if they practice dual agency.

Chapter 7: Coming Soon

If your broker wants to market your property as *Coming Soon*, they are really attempting to lead you into a dual agency situation. If you prohibit dual agency, the broker will become rather indifferent about the whole coming soon idea.

~~~

Another conversation:

Broker: So before I have you sign the listing agreement to sell your house, have you thought about marketing it as *Coming Soon?* What we'll do is stick a sign in the front yard and I'll put it up on my website. That way, we'll give your home a bit of buzz. But we won't make the home *active* (for sale) for two weeks. And we'll have all the possible buyers *dying* to see the place. Thirty days is even better, if you're not in a rush.

Seller: But what if someone wants or needs to buy it before the end of the 30 days? Surely, we don't want to lose a potential serious buyer?

Broker: Not to worry, you can show it to them. The local MLS does not allow me to do it. But I tell you what, I'll just pop by to check on you while they're here. And if they want to make an offer great. If we can work out a deal, even better.

Seller: Can we sell it if it is not *active?*

Broker: Well once we come to terms with the buyer and sign a contract, I'll change it to *active*. And then I'll immediately change it to *sold*. All kosher. And all wrapped up.

Seller: Hey that sounds really good, let's get this agreement signed.

Broker: Great, sign here. Oh, and I also need you to initial the dual agency language.

Seller: Yeah…we've been reading up on that, and we would prefer *exclusive representation*.

Broker: Really?

Here, the broker and sellers discuss the pros and cons of dual agency. Since there really are no pros to the seller, the broker whips out her best objection handling scripts. But these sellers have already read the previous chapter.

Seller: So yes, we want you to represent us as the sellers and only us. There, all signed and initialed. Now, when do we start the *Coming Soon?*

Broker: Well, you know, since you have prohibited dual agency, I cannot represent the buyer for your house.

Seller: Oh yes, we understand.

Broker: And if I cannot represent them, they will need their own broker.

Seller: Yes, we see that.

Broker: And of course, that broker will need to be paid.

Seller: Of course, but you did say that your total fee would be divided with the buyer's broker, right?

Broker: Yes but, we would need to wait until the end of the *Coming Soon* period for other brokers to show the house. Those are the MLS rules.

Seller: Well okay, but what about all the buzz? Surely, we'd still get all the buzz?

Broker: You know, the buzz is probably not as important as getting those buyers in here to see the place.

See the difference? It is really a question of whose buyers are we talking about? If the listing broker also represents the buyers in a dual agency situation, she keeps both sides of the commission. If the seller prohibits the listing broker from also representing the buyer, she only gets one side of the commission.

This *buzz* business, or however they're selling it, is really just subterfuge. What the broker wants, really wants, is both sides of the commission.

Chapter 8: Scripts & Objection Handling

If you get the feeling that a broker is reading from a script, they probably are. But most likely they are not actually reading. Oh no, they have memorized their scripts. Just ponder on this for a minute. And then go find someone genuine.

~~~

So what are these scripts we've mentioned? Well brokers have written responses to a whole host of issues. Some they write themselves. But most come from services they subscribe to. Yes, subscribe to our coaching service and we'll send you the top ten scripts for handling soon-to-expire listings. Then, we'll send you our top ten most productive scripts every month.

Brokers take these, perhaps customize them a bit to suit their taste, memorize them, practice them with each other, and whip them out whenever they talk to people. Anyone. Because the scripts are endless.

A couple of notes on these things. First, most of these scripts are about convincing people to hire them (Client Acquisition) or convincing people to do something that they really don't want to do. Brokers refer to the latter as objections, and the scripts are designed to *handle* or *overcome objections*.

And second, while the scripts usually have elements of the truth, they are designed to control the conversation. The broker knows your, say, three most likely responses, and has a canned response for each, leading the conversation in a way that benefits the broker.

If you are thinking that *normal* people are not so manipulative, I could not agree more. Normal people do not behave this way. But the real estate business is filled with this stuff.

Let's take some examples:

Seller: We can always come down in price later.

Broker: The higher a price is on a property, the less a seller needs to sell it…at least that is what brokers believe.

Seller: Will you cut your commission?

Broker: If a broker is so desperate that they don't value their own worth…is that the type of person you want sitting at the negotiating table trying to negotiate a better price for you?

Or,

Broker: Well, I have mentioned all the things I am going to do to market and sell your home…which of them should we forego in order to lower my fee?

I love this one:

Seller: We want to think it over.

Broker: I can appreciate that, making a logical decision is important…so tell me, what is it specifically that you're going to have to think over?

At that point, dear reader, I assure you, it is time to ask the broker to leave. Firmly.

If you get the feeling that I don't approve of the whole concept of scripts, you are right. Take the last one, above. Brokers are concerned that you may not call them back or may hire someone else, so they want to press you for an answer and a signature, right then and there. But surely a high integrity person would want you to think it over. Yes, even at the risk that you might not hire them. Using scripts demonstrates a lack of respect for clients and potential clients.

My examples above are simple. But these things can be quite elaborate: *If this, then that, if not, skip to step three.* If you are truly curious, just Google: "Real Estate Scripts." You'll find gobs of material on how to sound like a sleazy real estate broker. Yes, these things are sleazy.

And just think of the time involved to learn, memorize, and practice this nonsense. Time that could be put to more productive use. Maybe learning a new contract addendum or technology, familiarizing oneself with a new neighborhood, or reading a book on negotiation. Anything that might prove useful to the broker *and* her clients.

I also think there is a lack of self-confidence involved. I mean really, do these brokers not have enough confidence in themselves to hold up their end of a genuine conversation? I don't think they do. Is there any other class of professional who behaves this way? It is just not normal.

If you are in the business long enough, you will hear all sorts of often contradictory and sometimes weirdly perverse rationale for these things. Examples: Scripts are completely customer-oriented and solely benefit the customer; and scripts should be a continuous recitation from memory, so don't allow yourself to be thrown off by questions or other interruptions. And my personal favorite: Use scripts because you don't want to allow the customer to control the conversation.

Just imagine the mindset involved here: *Don't allow the customer to control the conversation.* The customer: You remember, that guy paying the broker a four or five figure commission. I can assure you these things are solely broker-oriented and solely benefit the broker. Yet the script-readers delude themselves that these things somehow benefit the customer, while at the same time minimizing any customer input or questions. And yet these brokers fail to see any contradiction here. Or maybe they do and they just don't care. If the word *steamroll* comes to mind you would not be far off.

Brokers would rather be good with scripts than actually competent, or even simply forthright. And they can be very good indeed. Very slick. Have you ever thought to yourself, this person has an answer for everything? But in fact, the best script-readers are so good, they are difficult to detect. Oh sure, if you've read the script, you'll know it when you hear it. But I don't keep up with these things and I certainly doubt that you do either.

But there is a tell. It is not foolproof, but it seems to work most of the time. When chatting with a broker, do you ask yourself: Is it just me, or is this person difficult to talk with? You might think that he is not listening to you. Or, you're not sure why, but it seems like the conversation is just a bit off-kilter. Maybe a little awkward or forced or tense, but for no obvious reason.

Well I am here to tell you, it is because you are not having a real conversation. Rather you are having a *scripted exchange*.

My advice: Kill it.

You don't have to be rude about it, but end the er... *conversation* as swiftly as you can. Well, yeah, unfortunately with brokers, you might have to be a little rude. Of course, it is more difficult on the phone or in person, but you don't have to respond to their emails or texts.

Like I said at the beginning of this chapter: Go find someone genuine. **If you cannot trust someone to have a sincere and genuine conversation with you, how on earth can you trust them with something as important as a real estate transaction?**

Chapter 9: On Malarkey

One thing that brokers are afraid to say to you: *I don't know*. I think they fear this will make them seem unknowledgeable or even incompetent. So what you get instead is some complete malarkey. I have seen buyers and sellers do the most ridiculous things based on this problem.

~~~

The Fear:

    Seller: Why is our house not selling?

    Broker: I'm not sure.

    Seller: What do you mean you're not sure? We are paying you to know!

The Result:

    Seller: Why is our house not selling?

    Broker: Hmm, maybe you need to paint the exterior.

    Seller: But we just painted it last year.

    Broker: I mean…the interior.

    Seller: Really? What color do you suggest?

The Truth:

    Seller: Why is our house not selling?

    Broker: You know, I'm really not sure. I think we've done everything and then some. We might just have to wait.

(Back to) The Fear:

> **Seller:** You know, we've waited long enough...You're fired.

The Lesson: Have an answer for everything. Or if you have to, make one up.

The Malarkey:

> **Seller:** Okay, we took your advice and painted the interior, but why is our house is still not selling?
>
> **Broker:** Have you considered new shrubbery?

Sometimes this is about pricing. And the broker just does not want to ask you to lower the price (again). There is an old expression in the real estate business: *Price cures all*. Sometimes you've done everything that can be done. If you are getting showings, your house is probably priced correctly and you just need to wait for the right buyer to come along. But if you have done everything you can, and are still not getting showings, odds are you need to lower your price.

One other scenario to watch for: Your broker is not getting the house sold, so you fire him. Then you hire a second broker, and at the same time substantially lower the price, and the house sells quickly. The first broker is a bum and second broker is a genius. Right?

The real lesson: Hire someone not afraid to tell you the truth, even if that truth is, in fact, *I'm not sure*. Even if the truth is: *We need to lower the price*. And if what they are telling you sounds like malarkey, it probably is.

Chapter 10: Licensing & Education

In North Carolina, it takes 75 hours of class time to obtain a real estate license. Meanwhile it takes at least 1,200 hours of class time to obtain a license to cut hair. Now either our stylists are incredibly over-educated or our real estate brokers are woefully under-educated. Make of this what you will.

~~~

I really have no idea how long it takes to educate future barbers and stylists. But in addition to how to actually cut hair, I can imagine that they spend time on health and sanitary issues. In fact, those probably make up the bulk of their class time. So I am not here to demean the amount of time required to obtain a cosmetology or barber license; I actually appreciate the effort involved.[3]

With that said, it is my contention that the complexities of the real estate business are at least as onerous.

And yet, here in North Carolina, we require less than one-tenth the amount of class time for an individual to qualify as a provisional broker. Granted, all brokers are then required to take an additional ninety hours of postlicensing education over the next three years. And until a provisional broker completes these ninety hours, he or she must operate under the supervision of a Broker-in-Charge. While requirements vary, North Carolina is similar to other states.

So my question: Is this adequate?

And further: Are the problems with the real estate business a function of lack of education?

---

[3] See the North Carolina Board of Barber Examiners and the North Carolina Board of Cosmetic Art Examiners. Other states have similar requirements.

My personal answers are *no* and *no*.

Let's start with the second question. Would more class time correct the problems and issues posed in this book?

Let's be honest, probably not. More education is not going to change the broker's two primary jobs and how they affect transactional competence. It is not going to change the financial incentives of the business. It could, I guess, make brokers more business and/or technologically savvy. But while the instructors could spend more time on ethics, class time alone is probably not going to change anyone's ethical disposition.

So if not education, is there another way to improve the business? The only way I know to genuinely improve the business is to educate consumers, and then for those consumers to demand better brokers.

But okay, back to the first question: Should we increase the amount of class time to obtain a license? Well, now that I have thought-out the second question, I think I want to change my mind on the first. I just am not convinced that merely increasing the hours of class time will achieve a better class of broker.

But like I said, make of this what you will.

Chapter 11: Continuing Education and Ethics

Questions: Do real estate brokers receive enough continuing education? And can adults learn ethics?

~~~

Here in North Carolina, the Real Estate Commission mandates that actively licensed brokers take at least eight hours of continuing education annually. This generally breaks down into one four-hour Commission-required *Update* course, and one additional elective. Other states have similar requirements.

Now, as the market, various regulations, and paperwork requirements are constantly changing, I find the *Update* classes quite informative. As for the electives, well obviously, some are better than others. And some instructors are better than others for any type of class.

If a broker is a REALTOR®, the National Association of REALTORS® (NAR) requires an ethics class every three years, which most brokers use to fulfill their required elective for that particular year. In recent years, NAR has changed the requirement from one class every four years, to one class every two years, to the current one class every three years. Yes, I know they are trying to find the right balance. But one does wonder if they are finding the whole exercise effective?

I can tell you, and it is just my opinion, that I am not at all convinced that adults can learn ethics. I do think children and adolescents can and do learn ethics. But think about how we go about teaching children *right and wrong*. It is a years-long daily exercise of example and instruction and correction, involving parents, family, teachers, faith leaders, etc. And children's books and stories, and *Mister Rogers* and *Sesame Street*. Right?

But can one learn ethics as an adult? I really don't know, but I remain quite skeptical. I think rather than *learn* ethics, adults *choose* ethics. We all choose whether to be ethical or not. But you decide for yourself.

In terms of the required ethics classes, I am sure that NAR would argue that something is better than nothing. And I suppose that is true. But I fear these classes are mostly for the sake of appearance. Ethical window dressing?

And yes, I do realize that our advanced society faces some complex ethical questions. Medical and military ethics come to mind. And of course, practitioners should study these. But let me assure you, the ethical questions in the real estate business are not that complex. They typically boil down to simple honesty.

So again the questions are: Is this enough continuing education? And would more help achieve a better class of broker? Here I actually think the answers are *no* and *yes*. In the pre-licensing classes, the students are totally new to the business, and therefore the subject matter is fairly basic. With continuing education, I find the material more useful to practicing brokers. And it falls almost entirely on the *Conveying Real Property* side of the business. If nothing else, these classes force the *Client Acquisition* brokers to, at least, listen to and hopefully take in some substance.

Chapter 12: The REALTOR® *Code of Ethics*

If the National Association of REALTORS® really wants to demonstrate the high ethical standards that they proclaim, they should ban single-agent dual agency.

~~~

The primary requirement for becoming a REALTOR® is agreeing to abide by the REALTOR® Code of Ethics. The National Association of REALTORS® describes it as *one of the first codifications of ethical duties adopted by any business group*.[4] It consists of seventeen articles describing REALTOR® duties to clients and customers, to the public, and to other REALTORS®.

But it is worth noting that, whatever NAR's ethical goals and aspirations for its members, they have not banned single-agent dual agency. And whatever the merits of the *REALTOR® Code of Ethics*, it does not ban this primary source of unethical behavior. Note: Not *one source* of unethical behavior; rather, *the primary source*. Yes of course, there are others. And on an individual basis, some much worse than the results of a typical dual agency. But in terms of widespread practice and acceptance, nothing comes close to dual agency. It is far and away the most prevalent and insidious ethical dereliction of the profession.

The *Code of Ethics* does a reasonable, even arguably comprehensive, job of addressing other ethical issues. In fact, I cannot think of any other problem that it fails to

---

[4] See the National Association of REALTORS® website:
https://www.nar.realtor/about-nar/governing-documents/the-code-of-ethics

address. Plus NAR does a great job of updating the *Code* as new issues emerge. And they are constantly emerging.

But other than requiring disclosure, the *Code* is totally silent on dual agency. And as Bill Gassett pointed out in Chapter Six, disclosure alone is wholly insufficient. In fact, disclosure gives the illusion of a high ethical standard that does not exist. I would go so far to say that even with disclosure, single-agent dual agency is incompatible with high ethical standards. You can have one or the other, but not both.

This is a huge ethical problem for the industry and it is totally ignored by the *Code of Ethics*. This is a dichotomy that can only be explained, I think, by understanding the acceptability of this clearly unethical behavior among brokers.

I want to be fair: Our earlier chapter on Dual Agency came largely from the website of REALTOR® Magazine. So this issue is alive and brewing in the organization. But really, it is not a complicated issue. It's just not. As Bill Gassett said: *It is a function of greed*. That's what it boils down to. It would simply take a little backbone to do the right thing. And if some members don't like it, well I assure you, we'd be better off without them.

Now I am a dues-paying member of the National Association of REALTORS®. I am also a member of our state and local associations. I am a member in good standing of all three of these organizations, and after publication of this work, I hope to remain so. Why? Well, most brokers, myself included, could not effectively practice real estate and conduct business without being a REALTOR®.

The REALTORS® provide the forms and the Multiple Listing Service (MLS). And regardless of what you think of this arrangement, the forms and MLS are very valuable indeed. And no other group is in a position to replicate either of these benefits. The REALTORS® also provide arbitration for disputes between members. A valuable service which, thankfully, I have never had to use.

My point is, on the whole, I think these organizations probably get more right, than they get wrong. Nevertheless, I see the dual agency problem as a huge lapse. And a lost opportunity to provide a leading ethical example. I call on NAR to ban single-agent dual agency.

Fellow REALTORS®, please join me.

Is there an Article 15 hearing in my future?

Here, fairly early in this work, I would like to quote Article 15 of the REALTOR® *Code of Ethics*:

> REALTORS® shall not knowingly or recklessly make false or misleading statements about other real estate professionals, their businesses, or their business practices.

As I said above, after publication of this work, I would like to remain a REALTOR®. And I think whether or not this book violates Article 15 is a matter of interpretation. But clearly, based on this Article, if they choose, they can and will expel me from their membership rolls. As I said in the Introduction: *I may pay for this transgression later.* And this is what I meant.

But in fact, Article 15 is a spurious ethical standard. I think it is intentionally written to be open to interpretation. For instance, here is one simple interpretation:

> It is unethical to question my ethics.

Oh come on, you say, that's crazy. Well, here's the same interpretation in a slightly more comprehensive format:

> REALTORS® (I am one) shall not knowingly (this work is quite knowingly written) or recklessly make false (a matter of opinion) or misleading (another matter of opinion) statements about other real estate professionals (other brokers), their businesses (their firms and business models and fees), or their business practices (their conduct and ethics, competence and integrity).

That is, it is unethical for a REALTOR® to question the ethics of other brokers. *It is unethical to question my ethics.* Let that sink in.

Now you ask, but how can you say that *false* is a matter of opinion? Well take the statement: *Single-agent dual agency is unethical.* Many brokers would label that *false*. Take another: *Many brokers focus on Client Acquisition to the detriment of Conveying Real Property.* Or: *Many brokers underprice houses.* Another: *Pushy brokers are stupid and lazy* (coming up in Chapter 15). *Most brokers do not compete on their actual value proposition* (Chapter 23). *Brokers prey on nervous and uniformed consumers* (Chapter 29). *Much real estate marketing is dishonest* (Chapter 32). How about: *Brokers hold open houses for dubious reasons* (Chapter 34).

While I would label all of these statements *true*, many brokers would label them *false*. Of course they would. And they will argue that these and other statements in this work are *knowingly false or misleading*, and therefore a violation of Article 15. Of course they will. Certainly if a broker deludes himself that dual agency is an ethical practice, he will have no qualms about labeling my statement *knowingly false* about his, er...*business practice*. The same is true for other unorthodox, unconventional, and nonconformist statements and ideas in this work.

So given this circumstance, I must grudgingly acknowledge that these are matters of opinion and scope. This is a work of commentary. Readers can certainly decide for themselves. But if REALTORS® wish to see them through a true or false lens, there is nothing to stop them. So I will not be at all surprised to find myself dragged into an Article 15 hearing.

Of course there are legitimate uses for Article 15. NAR offers a couple of legitimate *Case Interpretations* on its website. But clearly there is room for misuse, and more importantly, Article 15 can be used to enforce orthodoxy. And yes ironically, it can even be used to protect unethical behavior.

If the *Code of Ethics* is to be used to prevent a member from shining a light on questionable ethics, or even merely opening a discussion on ethics and integrity and competency, that is supreme irony indeed. And beyond that, surely it calls into question the real purpose of the *Code*. Because at that point, it becomes less, a code of ethics, and more, a code of silence.

So if I am to be removed, it would be less of an expulsion and more of an excommunication. For heresy. I would just point out that this is a book designed to improve the business. And if anyone can rebut any aspect of this work, they can and they should. Would that not be the responsible, and ethical, way to deal with it? Come, we will write our two narratives on facing pages, and the reader can be the judge.

So to my colleagues on the REALTOR® Professional Standards Committee, please read this into the record:

> To my fellow REALTORS®, I simply ask this: Do you not see the irony in removing a member for violation of ethics for writing a book on integrity?
>
> Remove me if you must, but shame on you.

Now I freely admit that this section is designed to be a preemptive defense of my work. But it is shameful that I should have to defend my work at all. It is unethical and dishonorable that anyone would use the *Code of Ethics* as a weapon to silence a discussion of these topics, regardless of what you think of the author's perspective. Surely this would be a betrayal of the *Code's* mission and your mandate.

Let me quote from the Preamble of the *Code of Ethics*:

> Such interests impose obligations beyond those of ordinary commerce. They impose grave social responsibility and a patriotic duty to which REALTORS® should dedicate themselves, and for which they should be diligent in preparing themselves. REALTORS®, therefore, are zealous to maintain and **improve** the **standards** of their calling and share with their fellow REALTORS® a common responsibility for its **integrity** and **honor**. [Emphasis added]

That is certainly the intention of this book. This book is nothing if not an attempt to *improve the standards and integrity and honor of our calling*.

But you might ask: Why not include this section at the end of your work? Because the goals of this book and the conclusions that I make are much more important and significant than the question of whether or not the REALTORS® kick me out. While this is an important question for me and my livelihood, it is merely a question in passing in our quest to find and identify competence and integrity in the real estate business. No, this question is unworthy of our conclusion, and belongs right here in our discussion on the *Code of Ethics*.

I hope the REALTORS® don't kick me out. But if they choose to do so, at least you are still holding this book in your hand or this work on your Kindle or other e-reader. That is something far more important.

So to the reader I would simply add: Ultimately, you *will be* the judge. The only judge that matters. Mark this page, and come back to it when you finish this book. What is your judgment?

Curious to know how it turned out? At the end of this book, in the *About the author* section, you will find my website.

I will keep you apprised.

Chapter 13: Words to Watch: Coach & Team

Words to watch: *Coach* and *Team*. Of course there is nothing inherently wrong with either of these words. But brokers shamefully use these terms to mislead potential clients about their role and how they conduct business.

~~~

Ten or twelve years ago, the word *team* really took off in the real estate world. Any broker with an assistant all of a sudden started referring to her *team*. Like headshots on a business card, some broker somewhere thought this was a good idea, and the herd followed. It is, I think, a sort of marketing ploy: Hire me, and you get not only me, but *my entire team*.

In our divided times, sports seem to be a uniting influence. We all watch sports and cheer for our teams, some of us play sports, and many of us encourage our kids to get involved in sports. Team sports and individual sports. Even in individual sports, like golf and tennis, kids play on a team. Kids learn the values of good sportsmanship, fair play, healthy competition, and hard work. And yes, teamwork.

So we all feel good about sports and teams. And these brokers want to tap into that: *I am not working alone here, I have a team. And just like a football team, each team member has a role. But the true benefit for you, dear potential client, is how we all work together to achieve your goals.*

And look, I really don't have a problem with that….

Assuming it's true.

But the most frequent experience our firm has dealing with real estate teams, is one of pure dysfunction.

A successful real estate broker is a much different animal than a competent manager. Let me put that slightly different: Just because one is a successful real estate broker, that does not make one a good manager. This managing business is a whole different skill set.

But here's what happens: Very successful brokers will hire people to help them. You expect that of course. First an assistant, then a buyer's agent, then a listing coordinator, then a transaction coordinator, then another assistant. You see how this grows. And rightfully so. If a broker is successful, he or she cannot do it alone.

Now to me, the definition of a smart person is one who knows or recognizes what he does not know. And I would expect a smart successful broker to recognize that as well: Hey, while I might be a successful real estate broker, I really don't know much about management.

And then they have two choices. Either acquire management skill or hire it out. Yes, they can turn some of their focus away from brokering real estate to managing people. Or, they can simply hire a manager.

Now, which one of these choices do you think they make?

Well I am very sorry to report, the answer is *neither*. They do not turn some attention to management. My God, that would take time away from Job Number One: Client Acquisition. And because they overestimate their own abilities, they also neglect to hire a manager.

The result is pure dysfunction.

Wait, I said brokers shamefully use the word *team* to mislead potential clients about their role and how they conduct business. But while these brokers may be incompetent managers, they *are* operating a team (if not *as* a team). So what did I mean by *mislead*?

Well, take two brokers, partner them together, and what have you got? A team. Married couple selling real estate? A team.

And then there's this: Take a solo broker, who wants in on this whole team shtick, but does not have the business. So what does she do? Oh heck, she's got a team too. She has the Broker-in-Charge of the firm where she hangs her license. She has the firm's receptionist and assistant and bookkeeper. Plus, she has her go to attorney, and her go to home inspector, and her go to handyman. All team members in good standing. So in reality it may just be Rachel Brown, Broker, but by golly, she promotes herself as: The Rachel Brown Team. Of course she does.

So hire a team if you like. But watch for both of these: Dysfunctional teams and illusory teams.

Now, briefly, about the term: coach.

Some brokers will refer to themselves as a *coach*, as in Jon Brown, your real estate coach. I guess the idea is that they are going to coach the buyer or seller through the process. And hey, maybe that is true. I suppose there are worse ways to describe what real estate brokers do.

But make no mistake about it, just like the *team* brokers, these guys want you to associate them with the feel good sports analogy.

Personally, I view real estate brokers less as coaches and more as consultants. What's the difference? Well to me it is a question of who is working for whom? Just a thought.

But hey, if you like the sports analogy, go with it.

Chapter 14: And Brokers Have Their Own Coaches

In sports, players will hire a coach to help them perfect their game. Some real estate brokers will hire a coach to help them increase their business. Now one might think that doing more business would help these brokers perfect their game. It does not. Sports coaches do not help players play more; rather, they help them play better. Real estate coaches do not help brokers play better; they only help them play more. And this is what these brokers want: Not better, just more.

~~~

In the real estate business there is a class of consultant that refer to themselves as coaches. Not real estate coaches in the sense we used the term in the previous chapter. But rather these people are consultants to the brokers themselves. They *coach* brokers on how to do more business. They are essentially, sales coaches.

Now these consultants and the brokers that hire them would argue, the coaches are far more than merely sales coaches. That in fact, they provide coaching on every aspect of the broker's business. So for example, you will hear brokers say things like: *You know, when my business got to the point that I needed a team to keep growing, my coach was just invaluable*.

But, we've already discussed the whole team shtick. It's often a bit of a gimmick. But to what end? Well, to increase sales of course. And this is a perfect example of what this coaching business is all about.

I would argue that the worst attributes of contemporary real estate brokers and how they conduct themselves come from this class of consultant. Don't get me wrong, the coaches advise, and brokers think and behave this way, because it works. It would be naive to deny that reality. But in my opinion these tactics, while perhaps successful, really demonstrate questionable integrity and a degree of shadiness. And certainly, a lack of respect.

Example: *Only show three homes at a time*. Wait stop; I actually agree with this sentiment. I mean, I might extend it to four, five, or six, but if you show too many homes at any one time, they all tend to run together. But then the coaches continue (I will start over): *Only show three homes at a time…then ask them to buy one*. Wait, what? Really? See what I mean? That tactic might work, but I personally question the ethics, not to mention the work ethic.

But of course the goal is quick sale, easy sale, so the broker can get back to *client acquisition*.

This class of consultant is primarily responsible for the scripts used in the business. But like I said at the end of our chapter on scripts: If you cannot trust someone to have a sincere and genuine conversation with you, how on earth can you trust them with something as important as a real estate transaction?

Well they teach and use scripts because they work. But that does not make them good business practice. It does not make them honest. Again: They are just not normal; not better, just more.

It goes well beyond scripts. There's an attitude to this training that I don't see in any other business. *Show them three houses and ask them to buy one*. It is condescending and disrespectful and belittling. In fact, I know of no other business that thinks so little of its customers.

As an example, coaches teach brokers to take control and be in charge of showing houses. If the buyer gains control of the showing process, not only is the broker reducing his chances of making a sale and earning a commission, but also extending the length of the sales process from days to weeks.

If the buyer gains control...? All hail the mighty broker! I'll tell you what: If there is anyone who should be in *control* of a six-figure purchase, it should be the buyer. To think otherwise is nothing short of despicable.

Another example, coaches teach brokers to call potential clients as often as they can, because *brokers don't lose business by being too aggressive*. Yes, there is a reason real estate brokers behave the way they do. They actually believe this is true. David Mamet's *Glengarry Glen Ross* springs to mind. *ABC: Always Be Closing*.

I close this book with a whole section on real estate negotiation. But let me point out here that as negotiators, brokers should never be aggressive or pushy. In fact, just the opposite. It is testament to the intellectual limitations of this class of broker that they actually believe this is a good way to conduct business. Now they would argue: *Well chump, say what you will, but it works*. But it only works if all you care about is acquiring clients and a rush to close; and you don't care at all about looking out for your clients' best interests. Yes, it works for that.

Instead, I would argue never rush to close. In fact, forget about closing. Allow the deal, any deal, to *come together*. Without pressure. *Well chump, you can have that attitude, but I'll gladly come in and steal your candy*. But as I will mention several times in this work, if you are reading this book, you are probably not going to be swayed by this sort of nonsense. Or perhaps you have done so in the past, and see now that it was a mistake. Pushy, aggressive brokers are not very smart, or competent. Choose smart over pushy every day. We are here, reader and writer, because this is a serious business. So let us be serious. We will have more on this in our next and last chapter in this section.

Not better, just more. And not even more for the seller, as in more money. Because these coaches spend a lot of time on how to get the seller to accept as little as possible. No, just more for the broker.

I am always just amazed by the lack of respect the coaches and their broker clientele have for potential customers and clients.

These guys sell their coaching services as subscriptions. They do videos and one-on-one coaching. They sell books and CDs and DVDs. They have events. You know, seminar type events, that look and feel like Amway conventions. Brokers attend, I'm told, because they are motivational. I guess like going to see Tony Robbins. And hey, if that is what these brokers need, fine. I just wish there was more substance to it all. And respect. My preference would be for brokers to spend time on something, anything, that would benefit their clients at least as much as themselves.

For instance, let's look at some topics these coaches do not discuss:

The latest construction techniques or the pros and cons of slabs versus crawl spaces or siding choices. Material facts or inspection and repair issues or wire fraud issues. Polybutylene replacement choices, sizing septic systems. Record retention and digitalization. Contract changes or escrow account requirements. 1031 exchanges. Short sale techniques or radon or mold. Dealing with Homeowners' Associations. Zoning changes. Municipal annexations. Unpermitted improvements. Reducing client risk. What home improvements offer the best payback. Strategies and best practices for offer and acceptance.

See a pattern? You know, the multitude of issues on the *conveying real property* side of the business. No, you don't hire a coach to learn about radon and mold and best practices. You hire a coach to learn about *client acquisition*. So don't let anyone pretend that these guys are anything but mere sales coaches with bad attitudes, questionable ethics, and no respect. Same for the brokers that hire them.

Before we leave this topic, what about negotiation strategies? Oh sure, the coaches may introduce some negotiating scripts. I can just imagine: *Objection Handling for Negotiations*. But in addition to demonstrating a low integrity activity, I hope I have convinced you how childish and frivolous and shallow all of this is. To me, it all just seems to have a quality of *unseriousness*. It reeks of unseriousness. Put a competent broker on the other side of a transaction and the lack of real skill and knowledge becomes all too apparent.

And these brokers could not care less. Because they are motivated, they are scripted, they are upbeat, they can manipulate, I mean handle, prospects and clients. And they *are* serious about these…er, qualities. But they are not serious about ethics or competence or acquiring competence or really, serving their clients.

Unserious. I looked it up: It said, see real estate coaches and the brokers who hire them.

Chapter 15: Pushy Brokers are Stupid Brokers

Aggressive, pushy brokers are stupid and lazy, and they will gladly sacrifice your best interests to put a quick and easy deal together.

~~~

Now I hear you: *I am selling my house. I need to sell it quickly. I need a go-getter. I need an aggressive, and maybe even a pushy, broker. I don't have to like her, I just need it done.*

Right? We hear this sort of thing all the time. And I understand it. I even sympathize with it. But I assure you, you are being hoodwinked.

Because what you see when you engage an aggressive and pushy broker, is how they operate on the *Client Acquisition* side of the business. And this tells you absolutely nothing about their competency *Conveying Real Property*.

Do not confuse *aggressive* with *hard-working*.

But for a moment let's assume that aggressive means hard-working. Well it is one thing to be hard-working at *Client Acquisition* and it is an entirely different thing to be hard-working at *Conveying Real Property*. Unfortunately, aggressive and pushy work on the *Client Acquisition* side of the business, and brokers can and do *work hard* at that.

But aggressive and pushy absolutely do not work on the *Conveying Real Property* side of the business. And be assured the *Client Acquisition* brokers do not work hard on this side of the business at all. No, they are much too busy for all the detailed rigamarole. For them, it is just something that they must get through as quickly and as easily as possible. Does that sound like hard-working? Heck, does it even sound aggressive? It is neither.

And to the extent that these brokers give *Conveying Real Property* any attention at all, they employ the same tactics that work for them when acquiring clients. But in fact, conveying real property runs counter to everything these brokers and their coaches believe. With their pushy scripts and their total lack of respect for their clients and their rush to close. As I said in the previous chapter: It is testament to the intellectual limitations of this class of broker that they actually believe this is a good way to conduct business. They are not smart enough to understand the distinctions involved and the different necessary skill sets.

I would call it amateur, but I think labeling this behavior *amateur* gives them too much credit. And they are certainly not amateurs at what they think is important, *Client Acquisition*. They are very accomplished at that indeed.

No, I think their attitude and behavior is much worse than amateurish. It reflects a total lack of regard for their clients and transactional competence. So what is that? Stupid? Lazy? Unprincipled? Unthinking? Self-serving? Shortsighted? Something else? It's all of this and more. You can decide for yourself. But whatever it is, it is done by brokers who do not truly understand the business, or do not respect their clients, or both.

Let's return to our seller: *I need to sell it quickly. I need a go-getter.* Well if that is the case, you want someone who will work hard and smart and fast to convey your property and protect your interests. Someone not afraid to get their hands dirty. That is not someone primarily concerned with acquiring more and more clients.

Conveying Real Property is just a lot more work and takes an attitude of delayed gratification that you will not find in aggressive, pushy client acquisition types. If they bring their aggressive and pushy attitudes to this side of the business, they are going to do you more harm than good, and take longer to get the job done.

Or maybe not longer. Because they will absolutely be happy to sacrifice your best interests to put a quick and easy deal together.

Please, don't fall for this charade. Want a gunslinger? Fine. Don't hire an unserious pretender. If you want a real gunslinger, you don't hire a rhinestone cowboy.

Rhinestone Cowboys, Gunslingers & George Baileys

Now we all know the term *rhinestone cowboy* from Glen Campbell's 1975 hit single of that same name, written by Larry Weiss. Weiss used the term endearingly to represent a country singer who had struggled and survived and finally found success. And we all admire that level of persistence and perseverance and hard work.

But whatever else *rhinestone cowboy* may mean, clearly it is a glitzy and inauthentic pretender. Ask any wrangler with dusty boots and grimy fingernails.

As for *gunslinger*, how have we traditionally used that term in business? An aggressive and competent hotshot.

Now we just need a similarly picturesque term for a quietly competent wrangler, not afraid of hard work or getting his hands dirty; never the hotshot, but consistently reliable, levelheaded, and scrupulously honest. Perhaps sometimes undervalued or underestimated? The Jimmy Stewart type. Hmm, if you will forgive the triple-mixed metaphor, I guess we could label these guys: *George Bailey*. Yes, the George Baileys.

So we have the rhinestone cowboys, the gunslingers, and the George Baileys. That's Americana. I do not want to overuse these terms; they are only get us so far. But used sparingly, I do think they help paint a picture of what we often see in this business.

Section Two:

Buyers & Sellers

Chapter 16: The Solid Brown Zebra

People have a preconceived notion about what a real estate broker should look like and sound like. If someone does not fit into their *idea of a broker*, they will not hire them. Competence and integrity rarely come into it.

~~~

So what is the stereotype of a real estate broker? Well she's coiffed and polished, slightly pushy, constantly on her cell phone, and I think most importantly, she talks a certain way. That is, in scripted language. But most people just think to themselves: Oh real estate brokers, you know, they all sound alike.

And let's be honest, it's a stereotype for a reason. I mean not a few brokers are walking caricatures. Yet, and here's the point, people hire them. Every single day. Too often, brokers are not penalized for even their obvious faults.

Why?

Because whether they like brokers, or the stereotype of brokers, people believe that is what brokers are or should be. To do otherwise would be like hiring a solid brown zebra. Even if that solid brown zebra is the Serengeti's best grass eater, he does not look the part, and therefore does not get hired for the role.

So people hire their *idea of a broker*. Competence and integrity rarely come into it.

And hey, maybe it goes well. Bingo, we all know it takes black & white stripes to be a zebra.

And if it does not go well? Well clearly, as a breed, zebras are dumb, or lazy, or dishonest, or just plain incompetent.

Don't be these people.

Chapter 17: The Pretense of Competence & Authority

It is extremely difficult to get good reliable information about brokers and the sales process. Oh there is plenty of information out there. But most of it is bad.

~~~

I have never met a broker who did not proclaim themselves to be a good negotiator. I close this book with a whole section on real estate negotiating, as it is or should be a core competency of a broker. But here, let me just address why brokers claim to be good at this skill set and why they are, in fact, not.

It's a marketing thing. Of course it is. Brokers cannot say to potential clients: *Look, once I have acquired you as a client, my heavy lifting is done.* Of course not. So when selling themselves to any potential client, brokers must present themselves as competent. Yes, ironically, competent at *conveying real property*.

What's the alternative? An honest broker would be required to say: *Look, I'm really great at acquiring clients, and I spend almost all my time on this. So I've never taken the time to study negotiation in detail; to really give it the thoughtful attention it deserves and demands. But don't worry, everything will be fine.*

So what they say instead is: *Look, I've been doing this for twenty years, and I have represented hundreds, or thousands, of clients. Believe me, my negotiation experience is second to none.*

Except it is not. Not only have they never properly considered or practiced negotiation, since this skill falls squarely in the conveying real property category, really, it is just something to get through as quickly as possible. So they can get back to making money…prospecting. It is just not important to them.

There is a broker in our market who is a top producer in terms of number of transactions and transaction volume. She is a genius at Job Number One: Client Acquisition. And I mean it, a genius.

In 2016, five years after the *Due Diligence Contract* was introduced in our state, this broker posted a video on her YouTube page explaining the concept of due diligence to the audience, and one supposes, to her clients. In this video, the broker claims that during the *Due Diligence Period* of the contract, *the seller has no control whatsoever* and *the total jeopardy is on the seller*.

This admonition is quite simply false. And it is no *small* false thing. An understanding of the Due Diligence provisions of the contract is an important negotiating advantage. I personally believe it is the most important, and I have a whole chapter on this in the Negotiation section of this book. Here, let me just point out: Through the amount negotiated as the *Due Diligence Fee*, the seller controls the *Due Diligence Period* at least as much, and arguably more, than the buyer.

Now it is not my intention to get into the weeds of the real estate contract. The question is, why would this top producer make such a statement?

Well she clearly spends all her time, effort, and money, on *Client Acquisition*, to the detriment of transactional competence. One might think that, with so many transactions, a broker would necessarily pick up some competence. But the real estate business does not work that way. I assure you, this broker is more than competent at what she believes is the only part of her job that really matters: *Client Acquisition*.

So if you hire a top producer thinking that if the broker does so much business, they must know what they are doing, you are correct. They do know what they are doing and they are experts at it: *Acquiring clients*. The rhinestone cowboy has no ambition whatsoever to become a real cowboy. He only hopes that you don't know the difference.

Transactional competence is something altogether different. Competence must be purposefully acquired. Competence is a choice. It is a choice of focus.

That video is still online in 2020. If you visit this broker's YouTube page, you will find many videos on any number of real estate subjects. And she speaks with such authority. On the face of it, clearly she knows what she is talking about. Right?

But this is no more helpful than picking a broker based on production. The fact that she sounds like she knows what she is talking about, does not mean that she actually does. I mean her video on Due Diligence appears perfectly authoritative. But this too is a marketing ploy.

When selling themselves to any potential client, brokers must present themselves as competent. Yes, ironically, competent at *conveying real property*.

Chapter 18: Ratings, Signaling, and Peer Reviews

Most people will do more research on what new toaster to buy than they will on which real estate broker to hire.

~~~

Okay, so what about referrals and client testimonials and Zillow ratings, etc?

Sure, have a look. But in the real estate business there are an endless number of ways to harm your client without them ever knowing. Promote yourself, acquire a client, do a lousy job for them, and the client is often clueless. Underprice a house and the client might just thank you for getting it sold so quickly.

The point is, many people really have no idea whether or not a broker has done a good job for them. Most buyers and sellers simply do not do this often enough to know one way or the other. I love underpricing as an example here. What is more important, a quick offer and contract, or the best offer and contract? Yet brokers continue to brag about quick sales because sellers do not realize it is a function of underpricing. Or maybe the broker lost a deal for a buyer because she did not know how to put a pdf document together. How would the buyer know? By the way, they left her a fantastic review.

So the ratings and reviews often come down to simply this: *I liked her.* Great! I am not saying to totally ignore referrals, testimonials, and ratings, but take them for what they are worth.

In economics, there is a concept called signaling. Firms and individuals signal their competence and their value in various ways. An individual may signal his or her ability level with an Ivy League degree and an extensive resume. A firm may signal its value with posh offices and pricing. Yes, most people believe that you get what you pay for. So, if a firm wants to signal that they offer superior service, one way they can do so is to simply charge superior prices.

Of course, over time, if the actual service provided does not match the superior prices, this will eventually catch up with the firm. But, it can be slow to catch up.

Let's take a break from real estate and look at another service business: Legal services. Don't worry, I am not about to compare real estate brokers with attorneys. I just want to look at how people shop for legal services.

It is largely referral based, right? We can ask our friends and family and colleagues for a referral. Or we can ask our real estate attorney if they know a good estate planning attorney. Now of course, this is very similar to real estate.

But then, we also use signaling: We go to the attorney's website and discover that she went to Harvard Law School. And before that she attended Vassar on a full academic scholarship. Right? And sometimes they will list their major clients. And we see that she is a member of the bar in our state *and* in New York and Delaware. We might learn that she argued and won a case before the state's Supreme Court, and wrote about it for some prestigious legal journal. Yep, there's the link. And finally, we look up her address, and find her office in an expensive office park, rather than in some walkup over a pizza joint.

Of course. But it largely depends on how important our legal issue is, right? And legal issues can be pretty important. And how much is all this going to cost? I mean, if it is a simple will, we may not pay much attention to all this signaling. But if we have complex estate issues, we might give it a lot of attention.

In the market for legal services, there is also the concept of *Peer Review*. Yes, attorneys will rate other attorneys they have dealt with. While every business, including legal services, offer some form of customer or client review, surely a colleague in the profession would be better equipped to offer a useful and informative review. A judgment based on the reviewer's own knowledge and experience and expertise. Now of course, it is not a perfect system. But whatever you think of it, it does add to our ability to find a competent attorney. Personally, I find them helpful. I just do not know enough about the law and the legal process to make an informed judgment myself. But if I see that an attorney has an AV rating[5], I sure feel better about engaging them.

Okay, so let's return to the real estate business. Yes, there is some signaling involved. Of course there is. But I submit to you that it is much less substantive than it should be. Let's be perfectly honest here: The primary signaling done by real estate brokers is their choice of automobile. Right? I will let readers judge for themselves whether or not this is an effective signal, but I think we can all agree that it is rather limited in its utility.

As for education and experience and major clients and all the rest of it, for the most part, this is completely lacking on the residential side of the real estate business.

And just like in the legal services business, whether or not signaling matters is largely dependent on how important or

---

[5] AV is the *Preeminent* peer rating by Martindale-Hubbell, which maintains and publishes a database of attorneys.

expensive the client's needs are. Maybe if the client is buying a $100,000 townhouse as a rental unit, well, it's really no big deal. But if the client is buying a $500,000 home to raise their family, I just wish (and that is all it is, a *wish*) that they would invest a tiny bit more time and effort beyond merely admiring the broker's car.

Now I mentioned peer reviews for attorneys. And sure, for most of us who are not attorneys, we probably know a bit more about real estate and the real estate process than we know about the law and the legal process. Nevertheless, I wish (and that is all it is, a *wish*) that there was some outlet for peer reviews of real estate brokers. I think that would be quite helpful, even for those of us in the business. I may be a real estate expert in my area, but peer reviews would help me select other brokers to work with, advise clients on out-of-area brokers, or brokers out of my field of expertise. After all, the biggest users of attorney peer reviews are other attorneys.

In any case, we only get so far with referrals, testimonials, and ratings; professional real estate signaling is of limited and questionable utility, and peer reviews are nonexistent. So we do need to spend more time and effort to determine broker competence and integrity.

And most of us, just don't. But in our next chapter, I will propose one way we might.

Chapter 19: How to Find a Competent Broker

If you want to find an honest *and* competent broker, ask them if they practice dual agency.

~~~

Okay, so then, how does one find a competent broker? How does one cut through the nonsense? Well I may not have a perfect answer, but based on years of experience dealing with brokers, I do have a theory:

> There is a positive correlation between competence and honesty.

I put it in the Introduction: Competence is a character trait and a function of integrity. I think an honest person feels duty-bound to be competent. Or, to be honest about their lack of competence. Or, would do something to become competent. I think it is also true that a competent person is more likely to be honest. Right? They certainly have less to be dishonest about. In any case, both honesty and competence spring from integrity.

At the end of Chapter Six, I suggested that if you wanted to find an honest broker, ask them if they practice dual agency.

So here, let me extend that advice: If you want to find an honest *and* competent broker, ask them if they practice dual agency. If nothing else, when you ask a broker about dual agency, it will lead to a conversation that will help you make a judgment on both their honesty and their competence.

But do not lead them. Ask an open-ended question: *What do you think of dual agency?* And then wait. Don't say any more, don't explain, don't clarify. If the answer is anything other than an immediate: *I do not practice dual agency*, then you have a problem. Do not allow them to answer you with a question. Not even: *What do you mean by dual agency?* Because they damn well know exactly what you mean. No questions at all. If you get a question, show them the door. And listen for scripted language. *I do not practice dual agency* requires no scripts. Anything else, anything, thank them for their time and show them the door. Only after a firm and early, *I do not practice dual agency*, continue the conversation.

Now the broker may respond with something to do with *designated agency*. You may remember we mentioned this, in passing, in Chapter Six. Designated agency is when two brokers work for the same firm, but each represent one of the parties. Do not be sidetracked by this. If the broker wants to get into the distinction between single-agent dual agency and designated agency, fine. Let them. But *I do not practice single-agent dual agency* needs to be a firm and early part of what they have to say. For example, they may respond with: *Well I don't do it myself, but if another broker in my firm has the other side, we do allow that*. That's okay, but it needs to be clear and fast. Because, really, it does not require anything more. Otherwise, the door.

Do not allow the broker the time to realize what you want the answer to be. Because then you *will get* the answer you want. Of course you will. No, it needs to be, it must be, firm and early, and preferably, immediate.

And let me add this: Most brokers who do not practice dual agency have strong feelings about it. Like me, they believe it is unethical. So often, if you happen to ask one of these brokers the question, you will get an earful. You will get your firm and early answer, and then some. That's okay; maybe you have found someone who is passionate about ethics and their fiduciary duties. You know, someone worthy of your business.

I hope by now that I have proven a primary thesis of this book: Competence is a choice. Brokers choose where to focus their attention. And as with honesty, the choice of competence is really a question of integrity.

As I mentioned earlier, if we want to improve the business, it is incumbent on consumers to demand better brokers. This starts with asking the right questions. And the dual agency question is pivotal.

Oh, and our top producer with all the authoritative videos: Huge practitioner of dual agency and coming soon. Of course she is.

Chapter 20: Anecdotal Advice

Be cautious of accepting and acting upon anecdotal advice from even trusted sources. *This is what worked for us and no doubt it will work for you too.* Well maybe. The problem is: Every transaction is different. And it can be difficult to extrapolate lessons from one transaction to another. The only solution to this is experience. And not one or two past deals. Rather, one or two hundred. But even then, plan on the unexpected.

~~~

There is just something about real estate: Everyone, and I do mean everyone, thinks they know more about it than they do. Don't believe me? Just ask them. If they've bought and sold one house, they will tell you all about it. If they have bought and sold three houses, they are certifiable experts.

Real estate is one of those topics that people just love to talk about. And look, I get it, for most people it is their largest asset. And they want to feel good about it. They want to be knowledgeable or at least feel knowledgeable. And of course, they want to share their knowledge and experience...with you.

This starts with the choice of broker: Oh you should really call our broker. She got our last place sold in one day. But it continues with how to price, and where to advertise, and what neutral color to use, because everyone knows you need to neutralize. It continues with what to offer and what to accept, and how much earnest money is enough, and of course what inspector to use, and well, it's endless.

And hey, there's no harm in it. So sure, listen to their stories, and sure, try to learn from their experience. That's what I do. And maybe you can pickup a nugget or two. I have. I mean if you get people talking about real estate, they can tell you some stories.

But just always remember that they are telling you about one experience, or three, or five, whatever.

Here's the thing: This property is different from that property. And this transaction is different from that transaction. And today is different from yesterday. And this town is…well you get the idea. The variables are infinite.

Here's my advice: Sure, listen to what they have to say. And if it makes sense to do as they suggest, well do so. But use your own judgment. And don't be afraid to say, or think to yourself, you know, I hear what he's saying, but that does not feel right to me.

Experience is vital. And there is no substitute for good judgment.

Chapter 21: Objectivity

Let's be honest, when it comes to buying or selling a home, people can be emotional, even irrational. Some brokers will pander to this. So try to find a broker that will inject some objectivity into the process.

~~~

Phone rings Saturday morning:

> **Caller:** Mr. Moore, it's Jim Smith, from the closing yesterday.
>
> **Me:** Oh? Yes Mr. Smith, I'm sorry we did not get to meet.
>
> **Mr. Smith:** Yes, well, my wife was pretty upset, and she could just not face you or your clients. So the attorney put us in a separate room.
>
> **Me:** Yes, so she said.
>
> **Mr. Smith:** Look, my wife is still pretty broken up about the whole thing…and I was wondering…er, I think it might help…if you could talk to her?
>
> **Me:** Hmm, er, well, sure…put her on.
>
> **Mrs. Smith:** [Sniffle] Mr. Moore, I really just want to tell you…well, I really just want you to understand…just how badly I feel you treated us.
>
> **Me:** Well, if it is about the price….
>
> **Mrs. Smith:** No, it's not about the price! Well *yes*, it *is* a bit about the price; it was lower than I was expecting.

Me: Hmm….but…

Mrs. Smith: But you know, our broker said we should probably take it. You know, she's a neighbor, well was a neighbor, and we've been friends since Jim and I moved to the neighborhood. I trust her so much. Thank God she was there for us. And besides, we'd already bought another home and we needed this one sold.

Me: Yes, your broker did saying something about a horse farm *before* we made our offer.

Mrs. Smith: That's right, out in Lee County. But as I was saying, I just feel that you treated us very badly.

Me: Well again, if it is about the price….

Mrs. Smith: No, I mean yes, I mean, it's not just the price. What really tore my heart out was your criticism of our home. You know, we were there for twenty years…raised our two kids there…and I just cannot believe the things you said…and how you acted.

Me: You mean with the repairs…?

Mrs. Smith: Well, there you go again with repairs…I can tell you, our home is in perfect shape.

Me: Well we did send you a copy of our home inspection….

Mrs. Smith: Oh that, well I couldn't be bothered with that. Besides I know more about that house than any inspector will ever know.

Me: But Mrs. Smith, the crawl space was so wet, the structure was covered in mold….

Mrs. Smith: That just cannot be true…I would have known.

Me: Well there are photos….

Mrs. Smith: Well never-mind that. I really just want you to know that I feel your behavior, well the way you treated us was just…just very…well, awful.

Me: Mrs. Smith I am sorry you feel that way…You do understand that I worked for the buyers, right?

Mrs. Smith: What difference does that make?

Me: Look, I think what you need to do is separate your sentimental feelings for your *home* from the business of selling your *house*. I am sure your broker told you that, or something to that effect?

Mrs. Smith: No of course not. She is my friend, she would never say something so cold.

Yes, this was an actual phone call. I hesitate to include this story because it seems so unbelievable. I don't really care if you hire a neighbor or a friend or a family member. But as we have discussed, find someone honest and competent. And as we see here, find someone objective. For your own good.

Now I am not saying that brokers should be insensitive to clients' feelings. Of course we should be sensitive. And this is an issue for some clients more than others. But clients hire us as advisors and consultants. Part of our job is to help clients make the best business decisions possible.

Brokers, do your job. Competence and integrity require objectivity.

Chapter 22: Real Estate Lags the Digital Age

The real estate business cannot be conducted via text message. When it comes to communicating with your own broker, you need to answer the phone and read and respond to your emails. If you are not adult enough to do this, maybe go rent an apartment.

Likewise, if you are a first-time buyer, it is time to learn how to use your checking account. You may be able to PayPal or Venmo some sellers, but the escrow agent and other vendors are going to expect checks or bank wires. Note that the contract most often does not allow for the time needed for your bank to mail checks. Alternatively, expect to get official checks from your bank. I know you are hip children of the digital age, but the real estate business is not. And for now, that's just the way it is.

~~~

Okay my younger friends, this chapter is for you. Let me just admit right up front, when it comes to technology, the real estate business is behind the rest of the world. We have discussed the fact that brokers are not the most technically adept people. But real estate is also a very legalistic business and a very regulated business. Any technology adopted has to meet these requirements. For example, as of 2020, the North Carolina Real Estate Commission makes no allowance for brokers to accept PayPal or Venmo-like escrow payments. Yes, I know that there are firms that will, but if they are acting as brokers, they are breaking the law (in my state).

Should you be able to Venmo your Earnest Money and Due Diligence Fee? And rent and security deposits and whatever else? Sure. But it is not really that the law is bad. It is just that the law and regulators are simply behind. Like you, I can only hope that they catch up some day soon.

Until then, you are going to need a checking account. And either order a book of checks or expect to go get checks from the bank when you need them.

It gets worse: This is a particular problem when you are moving to a new area, say out of state. Let's say you arrive for a few days to search for a place to live. And you find one. If you need checks for the *Earnest Money* and *Due Diligence Fee*, or security deposit and first month's rent, or whatever, but your bank does not have a branch in the area...what is one to do? I can tell you, sellers are not going to wait for you to return home, visit your bank, and mail a check.[6] That's just not going to happen.

So be prepared for this.

This is also true for rental units where a broker is involved. If you are renting directly from the landlord, they are not required to follow our state's Real Estate Commission's rules. So they may well accept some online payments. I know some of the large apartment outfits do this. But be aware, most landlords with rental houses use brokers.

---

[6] What about cash? Question: Can't we just visit any old ATM machine and withdrawal the necessary cash? Two problems. First, I have never heard of a broker or attorney or title company accepting cash escrow payments. Maybe it happens, but I've never seen it. I can tell you, our firm would never allow it because we want the accounting paper trail that only comes with a paper check. Why? Because we are subject to audit by our state's Real Estate Commission. And second, at least for real estate purchases, the amount needed may well be over your bank's daily ATM withdrawal limit or the ATM's owner-bank's daily limit. Heck, it may be more than several days' limits combined.

But if you can get the cash, you could walk into any bank and pay the non-customer fee to get an official bank check. I mean I think you can. Actually, I am not sure anymore. And in any case, this is not a good strategy on a weekend. So please, just bring a checkbook.

Now we have to talk about communicating with your broker. And I'll just be blunt here: There is nothing that will cause me to *fire a client* faster than one who will not answer or return my phone calls and respond to my emails.

Real estate is not a simple business. There are so many choices to make. Forms to complete; long forms. There are *if this, then thats* to decipher. As licensees, there are things that brokers need to be able to document that they discussed with you. Often email works best for this. But there are other times when nothing is better than a phone call. Your broker is probably not calling just to say *hello*.

Brokers cannot care more about your real estate endeavors than you do. But here's the thing, I have been in this business long enough to know that there is a lot that you don't think you care about now, but sooner or later, you will care about. And who gets the: *But why did you not explain this to me* question? The broker. If you are a first-time buyer, I would go so far to say, allow the broker to tell you what you should care about.

So if you want to text me that you are in traffic and will be a few minutes late, fine. But if we need to discuss the Inspection Report, take my phone call.

Now I know, if you are someone who can't be bothered with a phone call, even for complicated issues, you are probably not going to be reading a book on competence and integrity. On the other hand, if you go to the trouble to find a competent broker, get as much information out of them as you can. Make them earn their money.

Okay and finally, why include this chapter in a book on real estate competence and integrity? It is a fair question. But if a client, or even a potential client, cannot communicate with their broker, it will be impossible to judge competence and integrity, much less to insist on them. This whole business relies on effective communication. And we see enough problems in this area to warrant a brief discussion here. The same is true for the earlier bit about checking accounts and checks.

Section Three:

Fees & Business Models

Chapter 23: The Six Percent, Part One

Question: If you have a $500,000 house, should it cost you $30,000 to sell it? Set aside everything you know or think you know about real estate, and just answer this question with common sense. Please.

~~~

Do you know the old story about the guy with the very expensive foreign car? Well his automobile was not running quite right, so he took it to the dealer. Hmm, says the master mechanic, let's have a look. And with the owner standing right there, the mechanic opened the hood and turned a screw half a turn counter-clockwise. To the owner's genuine amazement, the car was back to its high-performance self. Then the mechanic says: That'll be $500. And the owner says, $500?! All you did was turn a screw. And the mechanic says, yeah you're right, that part of the job is five dollars. The other $495 is for knowing what screw to turn and how much to turn it.

Right? Yes, it's an old story and maybe you've heard it or some version of it. But what makes that story so good is the truth of it.

So is there anything comparable in real estate brokerage? Well look, there is art and science in this business of conveying real property. And I assure you, the knowledge and experience and expertise of a competent real estate broker is very valuable indeed.

Now of course some brokers are worth more than others. Of course they are. And full service business models are certainly worth more than limited service models. But what about the six percent?

Well if you have a $100,000 townhouse, I personally think six percent is fair. Or, close to fair. Maybe if you have some ultra-unique white elephant, six percent (or more) is appropriate. In fact, if you have a property with any unique set of challenges, six percent may well be fine. These might included deferred maintenance issues, a size that does not match the neighborhood, awkward layouts, etc.

But the question at the top of this chapter is: If you have a $500,000 house, should it cost you $30,000 to sell it? Let me add the word *typical*, as in a typical $500,000 house, in a typical $500,000 neighborhood. I think to ask the question is to answer it.

Instead let me ask a follow-up question: If you have a $500,000 house, what makes it $6,000 more expensive to sell over a $400,000 house? $12,000 more than a $300,000 house? Really?

Now I'm practical. I know that an oil change costs more on an expensive foreign model than on a Chevy. So sure, we all expect higher transaction costs for a $500,000 house than we do for a $400,000 house. I am not disputing this. But the question is worth thinking about. And I would add this: Just because we expect it, that does not make it necessarily so. Just ask former stock brokers.

What I would like to see in our business is more rational pricing, more thoughtful pricing, and certainly more diverse pricing. And more competition based on price rather than solely on who supposedly offers the best service.

What I really want to see is more competition based on *value*. Yes, yes, sure, everyone does. But have you ever considered the definition of value?

$$Value = \frac{Service}{Price}$$

Increase Service, value goes up
Decrease Service, value goes down
Increase Price, value goes down
Decrease Price, value goes up

Therefore, like both Nordstrom and Walmart, value can be found at any price point and at any service-level. And it is up to the consumer to decide if he or she values the service/price proposition of Nordstrom or the service/price proposition of Walmart. Or, maybe she values both for different particular needs, right?

I know, it's not a difficult concept. But in the world of real estate brokerage, this is like a foreign language.

Now yes, in the last fifteen years or so, the business has indeed moved in this direction. But even today, there are more Nordstrom brokers than Walmart brokers. This seems backwards to me. And what's worse, many of those Nordstrom brokers offer the subpar competence we have talked about. So really, they are only offering the illusion of high service.

Somewhere in the distance, I can faintly hear Glen Campbell: *Like a rhinestone cowboy....*

Chapter 24: The Discounters & Their Clients

On the other hand, if you hire a low-price discount listing broker or a buyer's broker who pays you part of their commission, there will be things that these brokers will not do for you. And that is okay. But you cannot then expect the broker on the other side to do them for you. So plan on taking a greater role in the entire process than you might otherwise.

~~~

Now as I mentioned at the end of the previous chapter, the real estate business has indeed moved in the direction of more diverse pricing and differing value models. Today we see limited-service models, entry-only models, and various discounted fees. Still to come, I hope, are fee-for-service models and hourly-billing models. And no matter what you think of any of these, they are here to stay. And we'll see more of them.

The discount models that we see the most today are flat-fee listings on the sell side and commission rebates on the buy side. The flat-fee brokers charge a set fee for a particular set of services. They typically have various packages for, say $500 and $1,000 and sometimes even more. But the whole point here is that they do not do everything. In particular, they most often do not receive and negotiate offers. Instead buyers or their brokers send these directly to the sellers.

On the buy side, the way it works is the broker is paid a commission (by the seller) and then credits back some part of that amount to the buyer. Typically as a credit at closing, but it can be a check directly to the buyer afterwards.

The particulars of these discount models are quite various and beyond the scope of this book. But needless to say, I'm all for them and want to see more of them.[7]

But could we return to our Nordstrom/Walmart comparison? Nordstrom is famous for its customer service. They offer personal shoppers, no-question returns, and would never dream of shooing a customer out at closing time. Walmart's customer service offerings are a bit less; but of course they offer large carts and never close. But here's the point: No Walmart customer expects Nordstrom service. Oh sure, they may get it occasionally, but no one expects it.

If you are a buyer or seller and you hire a discount firm, you simply must understand that you are shopping at Walmart. You cannot then rely on the other side's broker to make up the difference. So if you are a seller, don't expect the buyer's broker to teach you how to interpret the offer or advise you on the due diligence process. And even if she does, be careful, because she's working in the best interest of the buyer.

If you are a buyer with a discount (commission rebate) broker, you cannot expect the seller's broker to show you the house, come to your inspections, or pickup your checks. And they will almost certainly neglect to inform you of some much needed buyer-protection addendum.

Now, just like at Walmart, the brokers might go above and beyond for you. For instance, they might see you as a possible future client and want you to appreciate them. But

---

[7] For a brief but interesting discussion of the benefits of fee-for-service and hourly billing models, and how they might work, see: Justin Wolfers, *How to Get a Better Deal From a Real Estate Agent*. The New York Times, 24 October 2019. https://www.nytimes.com/2019/10/24/business/real-estate-fee-for-service.html

you cannot expect it and you should always remember for whom they work.

Now as we discussed in the previous chapter, value is subjective. Some people will choose Walmart's value proposition and other people will choose Nordstrom's. But unlike value, competence and integrity are objective standards. While they may sometimes be difficult to evaluate, and sometimes even hidden, these attributes are not subject to personal preference. We all want competence and integrity.

So just because a retailer or a real estate broker offer a certain value proposition, that does not mean they are competent and honest at providing it. Kmart offered a very similar value proposition to Walmart; but by the end, they were not very competent at delivering it. Wells Fargo offers a very similar value proposition to Chase, but in the last few years, it has come to light that Wells Fargo operates with questionable integrity.

I have dealt with numerous incompetent and less-than-honest full-service brokers. I have also dealt with extremely competent, high integrity discounters. The reverse is also true.

So pick your value proposition and then look for competence and integrity.

Chapter 25: Duty Shifting

One reason a seller, through his listing broker, agrees to pay the buyer's broker, is to compensate the buyer's broker for showing the property to the buyer.[8] As I mentioned in the previous chapter, if the buyer's broker refunds part of his commission to the buyer, there will be things that the broker will not do. In fact, some brokers will not show their buyers any houses. Rather, they will say, if you want to see a house, just call the listing broker. But why should a listing broker pay the buyer's broker AND do the buyer's broker's job? The fact that a buyer's broker does not keep all of this payment has nothing to do with the seller or the listing broker. And per MLS rules, the payment is still made in full. Some people have a difficult time with this; they seem to believe that the listing broker has a duty to the seller to show the property. This is most often not true, and certainly never true for *represented* buyers.

~~~

Let's continue our discussion of discounters. If the buyer's broker offers the buyer a commission rebate of, say, half of their commission, that means the broker gets paid at the 50% level. Right? Let's take an example. The buyer goes under contract on a $300,000 house. The buy side commission is

---

[8] It should be noted that the compensation to the buyer's broker for showing the property includes the time and effort to show *this* particular property, but also for the time and effort showing *other* properties in order for the buyer to narrow his choice down to *this* property. The fee is not only for the one hour spent showing this property, but also for the twenty hours spent showing other properties that the buyer did not select. In theory, this narrowing process is valuable to the seller, and sellers have traditionally paid for it. But think about how this affects the fee. Instead of paying for one hour of the buyer's broker's time, the seller is paying for more than twenty. Point is, this is not an insignificant fee.

three percent, that's $9,000. At closing, the buyer's broker gives the buyer a $4,500 credit. This is great for the buyer. It will pay all or most of the buyer's closing costs, or it will buy a fair amount of furniture.

But it is, of course, not so great for the broker, who just gave up half of his commission. But that's the deal that the buyer and his broker agreed to going into this process. I have seen brokers who agree to make, say one percent, and rebate everything above that to the buyer. It's totally negotiable between the buyer and his broker. As it should be.

So naturally, the broker will take a Walmart approach to customer service. This is pretty much what we discussed in the previous chapter. But I mentioned one thing that I want to pull out and discuss here: Showings. Specifically, if a buyer hires a discount broker, who is responsible for showing the buyer houses?

One way that the buyer broker will try to economize is by not showing the buyer any properties. Or maybe I should say, as few properties as possible. As I said at the top of this chapter, the broker simply advises the buyer to call the listing broker. And quite often this will work.

Now it may be argued that the seller's broker (the listing broker) has a duty, to the seller, to show the seller's property to any *unrepresented* buyer. But even this is debatable, especially when you consider the whole question of dual agency. The point here is that this is a discussion that should take place between the seller and the seller's broker. Maybe for example, discuss this along with a discussion of fees. Pay the broker six percent and he shows the property to anyone and everyone regardless. Negotiate a lower commission and they both agree to be more discriminating with the broker's time.

But one thing is beyond dispute: The seller is paying the buyer's broker to show the property to the buyer. Please think about that, and yes, I have the parties labeled correctly. Again just to be clear: The seller is paying the buyer's broker.

Again from the top of this chapter: The fact that the buyer's broker does not keep all of this payment has nothing whatsoever to do with the seller or the seller's broker. The buyer's broker is paid to show the house. How this gets done is between the buyer and the buyer's broker. And however it gets done, do not attempt to shift this duty to the other side.

Duty Shifting: This is a term our firm came up with to describe any attempt by a real estate broker to shift one or more of *their duties to their own client*, to the broker on the other side. We found that labeling this practice makes it more easily and immediately recognizable. Brokers: Try it, it works.

Now, buyer rebate or not, I have had brokers serving as buyer's agents call me and say: Hey look, I am in a continuing education class all day (or my kid is sick, or even, hey I'm at the beach), would you do me a favor and show your listing to my buyer? Keyword: *favor*. I have done this many times for brokers. All of us have.

The difference, of course, is one of expectation. And one of business model. That is, if you design your business model to have someone pay you AND do your job, well, that only works with the grace or naïveté of the listing broker. It also displays an extreme lack of competence and integrity. Or arguably worse, an indifference to these.

Buyers: If you hire a discount broker for a rebate, have this discussion with them. Look for a competent and honest discounter.

Listing brokers: Short of the occasional favor, I urge you to stop showing your own listings to *any* represented buyers. I assure you, this issue will expand if we let it.

Discount buyer's brokers, a proposal: Rebate whatever you and the buyer agree minus $X per showing. Where X is $25 or $50 or $100. Whatever you and the buyer agree. That way, you are compensated for your time (the reader should note, still compensated by the seller) and the buyer has an incentive to keep showings to a minimum. You could include some number of showings as part of your deal, and then charge X for any additional showings. Lots of room for creativity here.

Brokers, do your job.

Chapter 26: On Paying Buyer's Brokers

Even for full service, it is not difficult to find a broker who will list your property for a dramatically less-than-average sell side fee. The primary reason commissions remain stubbornly high is the amount that sellers continue to offer the buyer's broker. I think out of fear that brokers will not show their property, or will steer buyers away from it. But in this mature internet age, brokers cannot hide your house from buyers. Weigh the pros and cons, do the math, and then pay them whatever makes sense to you.

~~~

The real estate business used to be fairly static. A seller would hire a listing broker to sell his house. The listing broker would charge the seller six percent. The listing broker would then offer any other broker half of the six percent to bring a buyer. So the two brokers would each make three percent. And all was right with the world.

Then some broker somewhere decided that, yeah, I still do pretty darn good if I charge five-and-a-half percent. I will still pay the buyer's broker his expected three percent. And yes, I will only make 2.5% myself, but you know, that's not bad. And I am more competitive than other brokers, so hopefully I will get more business.

We all know what happened after that. The 2.5% has fallen all the way down to $500. And sure, you get what you pay for. But we've talked about that.

While the amount retained by the listing broker now varies dramatically, the amount typically paid to the buyer's broker remains stubbornly static: Yes, we will list your property *entry-only* [9] for $500, but our sincere advice to you is to pay the buyer's broker three percent, because that is what everyone else is paying. Or, we will give you a full service listing for one percent, but our sincere advice to you is to pay the buyer's broker three percent, because that is what everyone else is paying.

And look, at four percent total, that's a one-third discount off the original six percent. Not bad.

But this business of paying the buyer's broker a full (or traditional) commission is a holdover from the days when the buyer's broker was the one finding the houses to show the buyer. And sure at that time, sellers and listing brokers were very much aware that the buyer's broker could simply *overlook* any property and the buyer would never see it. So by golly, they made sure not to give the buyer's broker an incentive to do so.

But who finds the houses today? The buyer himself. And even if the buyer's broker happens to be the one finding most of the houses, I assure you the buyer is still looking as well. Today there is no possibility whatsoever of a buyer's broker hiding a house from a buyer.

So let's take an example using our typical $500,000 house. And let's say the seller is paying a two percent commission ($10,000) to the buyer's broker, rather than the typical three percent ($15,000). Is a broker not going to show the house because the seller is paying ten rather than fifteen? And if not, how is that broker going to explain to his client, a potential buyer for the house, that $10,000 is not enough?

---

[9] Entry-only listings means the listing broker will enter the property into the Multiple Listing Service (MLS) only. The broker provides no additional services.

But brokers can be pretty brazen. The broker could say, well remember Mr. Buyer when you hired me, I told you that I charge three percent. And that if a seller paid me less than three, that you, as the buyer, would have to pay me the difference. So, if you buy this house, you will have to pay me $5,000 at closing.

Let's stop here for a question: Are brokers in fact having this discussion with their buyers?

Well for the most part, no, they are not…unless and until this situation arises. So it is at that point, after the house has been found, that the broker must explain to his buyer that, no, $10,000 is not enough. Awkward.

But it is possible. However, I submit that the following is at least as likely:

The buyer's broker says to himself, you know, $10,000 is a pretty decent commission; I think I'll just take that and be happy with it. Sure, I'll mention it to my buyers if there is an opportunity to do so without being crass. And maybe the broker also thinks: Besides, I have my buyer's current house for sale, so I'll get paid on that as well.

Right?

So sellers, if your listing broker suggests a five percent total commission (two percent to the listing broker and three percent to the buyer's broker), you might consider paying both brokers at the two percent level. And yes, the price point of your house is an important factor in this consideration.

Like I said: Weigh the pros and cons, do the math, and then pay them whatever makes sense to you. There is no need to blindly pay whatever is *typical* or even what your broker says you *must*.

Now one thing to watch for here: Most real estate contracts include a provision for *seller-paid buyer expenses*. So the seller may well be adamant that he is only going to pay the buyer's broker two percent. Nevertheless, the offer may include a provision for the seller to pay some of the buyer's expenses. Maybe the buyer asks for, say for example, one percent of the *Purchase Price*. Then, at closing, the buyer uses that money to pay the other one percent of the buyer's broker's fee. Just be aware of the possibility and know that this figure is negotiable like everything else. And this figure is often zero.

Another possibility: After you negotiate the contract, the buyer asks: Look I really need to pay my broker more, could we raise the *Purchase Price* one percent and add one percent to the *seller-paid buyer expenses*? Sure, why not? Because at the end of the day, all the seller should care about is his net. But in this case, just be aware that the property may not appraise for this new *Purchase Price*. So if you then agree to lower the *Purchase Price* to meet the appraisal, just make sure you also lower the seller-paid expenses.

But here, we are getting more into the weeds of the contract than is the intent of this book. But that is okay; it is, I hope, another demonstration of the value of competence and integrity.

Before we leave this topic, could we briefly discuss paying the buyer's broker even less? Returning to our $500,000 example, what if the seller says, I can only afford to pay (or I am only willing to pay) the buyer's broker one percent? That is $5,000. I think at that point, it is again worth asking: Is that enough? I am not going to answer this question for you. It is entirely personal preference. I will tell you that, like almost all brokers, I have often worked for commissions less than that amount. And on properties much more difficult to sell than a typical $500,000 home.

Just note that one percent of a million dollar home is a lot more than one percent of a one-hundred thousand dollar townhouse.

Just as we discussed earlier, I am in favor of more thoughtful pricing, more diverse pricing, and more value pricing. Maybe this leads to flat fees or tiers of flat fees (for both sides). Whatever. But charging a static six percent (total) or three percent (buy side) begs the question:

What is this worth?

Chapter 27: A Coming Clash of Discounts

In time, the buyer's brokers might have to accept the discounts all too common on the list side today. This would be a big change. Leaving little or nothing to rebate to the buyer.

~~~

So we have talked about discount brokers on both the list side and the buy side. And how the buy side discount works is with a buyer rebate.

For now, this rebate is somewhat guaranteed because sellers are reliably continuing to offer that *typical* three percent to the buyer's broker. The money technically moves from the seller to the listing broker to the buyer's broker to the buyer. But arguably this is tantamount to an involuntary money transfer from the seller to the buyer as an inducement to buy the house. Stop and think about that for just a moment.

But what if the seller says: Hey wait a minute, we just negotiated a five percent lower *Purchase Price*, why should I give the buyer another 1.5%, in cash, on top of that?

Good question!

Well surely once a buyer's broker has been paid, he has every right to do whatever he wants with his money, including giving some of it to his client, the buyer. Right? Of course.

But what if the seller says I'll pay the buyer's broker some reasonable fee, perhaps exactly what I am paying my own listing broker. But I will not pay him so much that he has enough money to give part of it away to the buyer.

What would that look like?

Well, I don't think much would change on the listing side. There, the fees already vary from $500 to three percent or more, depending on who you hire and what they do.

But now let's look at the buy side, with a very typical five percent total listing as an example. The listing broker keeps two and pays out three to the buyer's broker. But the seller says: No, I'll pay both sides two percent and no more. Well, the buyer's broker then has a dilemma. The buyer is expecting a 1.5% credit at closing (or whatever the discount deal), leaving the buyer's broker 0.5% for his time and effort.

So instead, maybe the buyer's broker will again offer the buyer half. One percent to the broker and one percent credit to the buyer. That might work for a $500,000 house. But what about a $150,000 townhouse? I don't know.

And what if the seller says, I'll pay three percent total…the two brokers can split it. Well again, it might work for a $500,000 house.

Think this is unrealistic? Some time ago, a broker in our firm listed a house for three percent total. She paid out 2.4% (typical in our market) to the buyer's broker and kept 0.6% for herself. Certainly not fair; but her fear was that other brokers might not show the house if she paid out any less. And the price point of the property was high enough that she was okay, if not thrilled, with the 0.6%.

But as we have discussed, in this mature internet age, I think this fear is misplaced. Brokers can no longer hide properties from their buyers. So today, I would strongly encourage our listing broker to split the three percent in half. If that is not enough for the buyer's broker to show the house, let him explain that to his buyers. If there is not enough money for the broker to offer a rebate to his buyer *and* still make a living...well this is a matter to be worked out between the broker and his buyer.

My take: This process should not be a *money transfer in disguise*. Since the seller is paying the commissions on both sides, the seller should reasonably benefit from the discount on both sides. As far as I am concerned, this should have always been the case. It has only been the lingering fear that buyer's brokers would not show the property that has allowed the whole buyer rebate form of discount to exist in the first place.

Just think about that. Sellers are paying buyer's brokers so much above and beyond what is actually required, that the brokers have enough to pay (rebate to) the buyer.

So in time, the buyer's brokers might have to accept the discounts all too common on the list side today. This would be a big change. Leaving little or nothing to rebate to the buyer.

And if the buyer's broker is not willing to accept these discounts, then he will have to ask the buyers themselves to pay part of his fee. So not only could the buyer rebates disappear, but the buyers may well have to start paying their own broker.

Time will tell. I am really not sure what the future holds, but it will be interesting to watch. But again, it seems to me that what the business needs more than anything is more rational pricing and more competitive pricing.

Chapter 28: iBuyers

As for the so-called *iBuyers*, they offer convenience and expediency, not economy. They buy low, sell high, AND charge the seller a fat fee for their service. Sure, it can be a legitimate alternative, but I suggest you do the math.

~~~

Here is the iBuyer model as I understand it:

- Purchase non-marketed properties for less than fair market value.
- In return, offer the sellers convenience and expediency (no showings and expedited & flexible closings).
- Charge the sellers a six – seven percent *service* fee.
- Sell the properties at or above fair market value.

If they can net a five percent return on investment, that's not too shabby. But then, if they can use their funds to do this, say on average, three times a year, that's a 15% ROI.

At this point they are paying buyer's brokers. But surely, as they gain market share and confidence, they will drop this expense and may even pull out of the Multiple Listing Service (MLS) entirely. That would certainly be my goal. That's another 2 – 3 points per cycle to their ROI.

And similar to the MLS, what's to stop the iBuyers from signing their own syndication deals with Zillow, Trulia, Realtor.com, even Craigslist, etc.? Thereby further reducing their dependence on the MLS.

And here's another question: If they withdraw from the MLS, what part of their business model would require a real estate license? My guess is they will drop that as well.

It seems to me that they have captured a niche of sellers who care less about representation and realizing the full fair market value for their property, and more about convenience and expediency. How long before they try to find a similar niche among buyers? The Opendoor website makes it look like they are moving in that direction. I think the younger crowd would eat that up like cannabis cupcakes. Think *no-hassle* pricing and all expenses included, or something to that effect. And they already have the inventory to offer potential buyers.

Now my view of the iBuyer business model may be somewhat cynical. But I fully acknowledge how popular this model has become. In 2019, Opendoor, the biggest iBuyer player, was the market leader in my county with over four percent of total listings sold.[10] Evidently there is a sizable market for this model.

It should be noted that 2019 was a seller's market with steadily rising prices. So a question I have is will the iBuyer model work with falling prices or in a buyer's market? Only time will tell.

Now one final thought about iBuyers. Even if their business model will not work in different market environments, does their current success not tell us something about consumer attitudes towards our industry? For instance, sometimes the

---

[10] According to the Triangle Multiple Listing Service (TMLS), there were 21,470 closed residential sales in 2019 in Wake County, North Carolina. Of those, 906 were Opendoor listings. This figure popped to just under six percent in the first quarter of 2020. And of course, there are other iBuyers.

price the iBuyers pay is substantially below fair market value. And yet, people still sell to them. So I cannot help but ask: Do these sellers hold real estate brokers in such low regard that they are willing to take substantially less for their property in order to avoid dealing with brokers at all costs? I mean, is it really, only, a question of hassle and convenience?

I talk to brokers. And uniformly, they say that for sellers it is a question of buying another home without a sales contingency (because in this market, buyers just don't have to accept them). And brokers add that many of the iBuyer sellers are in financial difficulty, and want a quick sale to avoid foreclosure. But clearly neither of these factors are true for all of these sales. I mean just look at the numbers.

So are brokers deluding themselves about what is going on? Are we witnessing a fundamental shift in market attitude? I think these questions are worth some consideration. I cannot help but wonder: Have we, as an industry, proven ourselves unworthy of these sellers?

Give this some thought as we continue.

Chapter 29: The Six Percent, Part Two

There is a firm here in our market that always charges a full six percent commission, nothing less. As buyer's brokers, when we deal with a property listed by that firm, we know we are dealing with an unsophisticated seller. Not savvy and perhaps even irrational. The kind of person who buys shoelaces at Neiman Marcus, because, you know, they're better.

Did you know that Warren Buffett's Berkshire Hathaway is one of the biggest real estate brokers in the country? Why? Because it is very profitable, especially at the six percent level.

~~~

As discussed earlier, I believe that Nordstrom's offers a particular value proposition. But even in 2020, there are more Nordstrom brokers than Walmart brokers. Why is this?

Well brokers know how profitable the business is, or can be, at the six percent level. It is not that they are all making a lot of money. Not by far. But brokers continue to believe that the path to riches is paved with six percent commissions. The problem for most brokers is that they simply do not do enough transactions to make a decent living, even when charging six percent.

I will admit that the real estate business is not easy. And sometimes we all believe, that even at six percent, we are underpaid. Sometimes. But there are other times when brokers cannot believe how much they are paid for a simple transaction. Again, sometimes.

In most businesses, pricing is an important consideration. Want to increase sales, look at your pricing. Of course, this is more true for commodity type businesses than for businesses differentiated by features or specifications or brand.

And here's the problem: Brokers like to think of themselves as offering a differentiated product. But differentiated from what? Well, other brokers: *I charge six percent because I am worth it*. You'd think they were in a L'Oréal commercial. And yes, arguably, a Lexus is worth more than its Toyota cousins. But certainly *perception* is part of the equation.

However, the Toyota Corporation sells a lot more Toyotas than Lexuses. The problem with the real estate business is that everyone wants to be a Lexus. Or pretends to be a Lexus. And even if they are not working, they maintain their Lexus pricing. This only works as long as the customers allow it...or, don't understand it.

I will tell you what many brokers will never admit: Many of the services offered are commodities and should be priced as such. And as we have discussed, many brokers offer only the illusion of Lexus-level service. Their value proposition is minimal. This certainly applies to almost all real estate marketing. Heresy, right? But it is true. We'll come to this in the next section.

Also, and there's no getting around it, this industry dynamic involves an element of work ethic. Or lack of work ethic. It is easy to get fat and lazy at six percent. If the industry average commission was dramatically reduced, brokers would have to really hustle. There's a lot more hustle at Walmart selling household goods than there is at Nordstrom selling high-end handbags. Now sure, Nordstrom has luxury offerings and a refined atmosphere and unmatched service. But what you have in the real estate business is Walmart brokers waiting for (and insisting on) handbag shoppers. They need to cut their prices, roll up their sleeves, and get to work. Yes, really.

I also think that reduced commissions would lead to a more professional class of broker across the board. With six percent commissions, what you find is many marginal brokers remain in the business who would otherwise have to find a real job. If we dramatically reduce commissions, these people would be forced to leave the business. Those remaining would be the true professionals.

But the real question posed at the top of this chapter is: Why do sellers continue to hire these brokers? It is, I think, a combination of factors that we've discussed. The pretense of competence and authority. The widespread, and often valid, stereotype of brokers. And the illusion of high service.

There is also an element of fear. Some sellers fear that if they hire the wrong broker, the broker might make an expensive mistake that the sellers cannot afford. I get that. But brokers prey on this fear. So many of them are little more than snake oil peddlers preying on the nervous, uninformed, and credulous consumer.

So with this book, I hope to convince you that six percent does not guarantee competence or integrity. In fact, it might even reduce these sought-after qualities. I have mentioned this a couple of times and I will again here: If we want better brokers, the only way we are going to get better brokers, is for consumers to demand better brokers. Please.

Sure, you can find value at six percent. But the real differentiating factor is transactional competence. Insist on it.

Chapter 30: The Future Will Be Online

There is so much money at stake that the traditional players are not going to be the ones to introduce radical changes. Rather, change will have to be imposed on the industry from the outside. It can be done and it is overdue. But I don't see anyone doing it. The insiders have too much to lose and the outsiders never seem to take the time to truly understand the business. Or they get co-opted by the traditional business. Take the two most prominent as examples. Zillow is, now, primarily an advertising platform for the traditional players. Redfin is, now, a fairly conventional brokerage with a fancy website.

What the Silicon Valley whiz kids need to understand is that there is no part of the process that people will do without. Very few people are going to buy a house without: Seeing it and alternatives, researching an offer price, negotiating the best possible deal, generating an enforceable contract, having it inspected, appraised, and if necessary, re-inspected, etc. So as cumbersome as the process may be, for any new model to be truly successful, the process must be maintained.

~~~

Allow me put an idea in front of you. Start with a company like Zillow, a firm that has a database of all residential properties in the United States. To that, we add a calendaring system for showings and other appointments. And we add a form completion package that works like TurboTax. For those of you who have never seen or used TurboTax, the software simply asks you a series of questions, and using your input, at the end produces the complicated tax forms. No training required; the system walks you through it.

Then we add an online valuation service. Using the property and sales database that the firm maintains, this system could produce an estimate of value for any property. But unlike Zillow's famous, or infamous, *Zestimate* figures, this system would have an *Advanced Customization* option. Here, users could (optionally) make changes to the subject and comparable properties, and make adjustments – Until they themselves are satisfied with the veracity of the result. Again, like TurboTax, the system walks the user through the process. No specialized training required. In other words, an online Comparable Market Analysis (CMA) that, with user input and adjustments, actually works.

So a seller, using this integrated valuation feature, could price their own property, list it for sale, and specify showing times that they are available to show the property themselves. Buyers can search and schedule showings directly with the seller. Then the buyer can do a bit of research also using the valuation feature (again with his or her own optional input), produce an offer using the integrated form completion feature, and submit it directly to the seller. The website could then offer a nifty back-and-forth negotiation tool. Once an agreement is reached, any monies due are transferred from buyer to seller using a PayPal-like feature. If money needs to be escrowed, this feature can transfer funds to local *recommended* attorneys or title companies.

Finally the two parties return to the integrated scheduling system for all due diligence related requirements and of course to schedule the closing. If repairs need to be negotiated, the forms and negotiation tools remain ready to be of assistance. Recommended attorneys, inspectors, and contractors are also available in the scheduling system.

Sure it could be some variation of this, but you get the idea. What I find most interesting about this Zillow-plus model is that there is no science fiction involved. Not even future tech. Everything discussed above could be done today. With the right vision and a lot of money.

But I don't think it will be Zillow that does this. While they are best positioned to put this together, they have proven time after time that they do not have the necessary vision. They seem to have no vision beyond providing an admittedly lucrative platform for brokers to advertise, and have no interest in alienating their golden goose.[11]

Zillow reminds me of Xerox PARC with their GUI/mouse combo. They did not know what they had. Then along comes Steve Jobs. That's where we are, I think; waiting for our Jobs. But someone *will* put this together. Here's a prediction: Whoever does this and gets it right will be the next Steve Jobs.[12]

Finally, I don't think the future will be broker-less. Perhaps it could be for some savvy players. But while TurboTax works for some, CPAs are still quite busy. And a system like the one described above could easily integrate real estate brokers.

---

[11] It should be noted that Zillow owns a company called DotLoop, which operates a forms and transaction management platform, very popular with brokers. The question is, does Zillow have any plans to open that platform directly to buyers and sellers? It would not make sense to do so without everything else we discussed here. But assuming they are not complete idiots, one does wonder if they can envision this sort of future. Again perhaps they simply do not want to alienate their current broker advertising clientele. But maybe they have a secret room in the basement where they are working on this. I certainly like to think so.

[12] The researchers at Xerox PARC (Palo Alto Research Center) knew exactly what they had. It was the Xerox executives who failed to see the GUI/mouse potential. It is interesting to point out that as of this writing Apple is the most valuable company in the United States and Xerox is a shell of its former self.

For instance: *Are you stuck? Need some advice? We have local brokers on call.* You see the point.

We all need to prepare for this now; it's coming.

Chapter 31: For Sale By Owner (FSBOs)

Yes, you are perfectly capable of selling your own property. This is not rocket science. The reason you hire a broker is not because you cannot do it. Rather, the reason you hire a broker is to save yourself time. The time to do it, but also, the greater amount of time spent learning how to do it.

However, many and perhaps most FSBO sellers overestimate their real estate knowledge. And therefore do not take the time to learn the intricacies of the market and the process. Brokers and savvy buyers take advantage of their hubris.

~~~

Let's start with the good news. In the previous chapter we discussed the coming future where online systems provide For Sale By Owners a platform that basically walks the seller, and the buyer, through the whole process. Right through to the closing. I have no doubt this is coming. However, it is not here yet. But sellers can use currently available technology to make the FSBO process easier than it has ever been.

In the past, one of the primary reasons to list your home for sale with a real estate broker was to gain access to the local Multiple Listing Service (MLS), the formerly print and now online database of all available properties, maintained by your local REALTOR® association. Why was this so valuable? Well, if you put a For Sale by Owner sign in the front yard, how many people are going to see it? But if every local broker, with active buyers in your vicinity and for your type of house, can easily find it, the odds of a sale were much greater. And make no mistake about it, this is still true today.

But today, the local MLS has a competitor: Zillow. And no matter how Zillow thinks of themselves, or how they describe themselves, they are, in fact, a private, online MLS competitor. Yes, today, a seller can go to Zillow, claim their property, add some photos and copy, and change the status to, you guessed it: *For Sale by Owner*. So today, while FSBO sellers still do not have access to the local MLS, they do have access to the next best thing. And every buyer I have met in the last five years was all over Zillow. In fact, as I have mentioned, brokers no longer find homes for buyers; the buyers are finding the houses themselves. Using Zillow and other similar sites.

Okay, now the not so good news. So yes, sellers can get their property in front of active buyers. But guess what? Almost all of those buyers have real estate brokers that want to be paid. So sellers, you will get this call: *Hey, I'm a broker and I have a buyer who found your home on Zillow; I'm calling to find out if you will pay me as their buyer's broker?*

Now the system I described in the previous chapter does not yet exist. There is no online platform, that I am aware of, that will guide the buyer and the seller through the process. So I would encourage sellers to agree to pay the buyer's broker. While always remembering that the buyer's broker works for the buyer, he or she can be useful to the seller as someone with a vested interest in walking the buyer through the process. Plus, more often than not, the seller needs some guidance to get through the process as well. While the buyer's broker does not work for the seller, the broker will help the seller through the process because that is the only way that the broker will get paid.

And by taking advantage of this, the seller has cut his real estate commission in half.

But at this point let me return to the top of this chapter. Sellers need to be cognizant of how much they know and don't know about the process. Sure, the buyer's broker will keep everything moving forward. But they will not insure that the seller gets the best deal. Of course not; they work for the buyer. The buyer's broker's first goal is to get paid, but their second goal is to take care of their client, the buyer.

Now a complete discussion of the FSBO process and how to navigate it is beyond the scope of this book. In fact, I could write a separate book on this subject alone. But I would like to return to the original phone call from the buyer's broker: *Will you pay me as the buyer's broker?*

Let me revise my recommended response. Instead of a straightforward *yes*, I suggest the seller say: *It does not matter whether I pay you or not; in any offer from any buyer, I am only going to be looking at my net.* Here we put the buyer's broker on notice that we, the seller, know that we are deducting our payment to the buyer's broker from the *Purchase Price*. So, the response to the buyer's broker's phone call is not: *No.* That would halt the process before it begins. But it is not exactly *yes* either. Rather, it is: *Yes, but I know how this works.* And then, when an offer comes, you need to negotiate with this in mind: I see you are offering $300,000, but as you know Mr. Buyer's Broker, that is only $291,000 to me.

One other really good response: *Well Mr. Buyer's Broker, I tell you what, I'll split your fee with the buyer.* To me, this is eminently reasonable. This way, the seller cuts his total real estate commission by seventy-five percent; down to around

1.5%. Be sure to add: *But I am only going to be looking at my net* (because this is still true).

Now, that's the first phone call that a FSBO seller will receive. Let's move to the second: *Hey, I'm a broker and I want to list your property.* They are soliciting your business to become your seller's broker (or listing agent). They will most often break out their best scripts for this phone call: *Hey, I was just wondering how it's going? Would you like some help getting more buyer interest? Would you like me to show you how to net more?*

Remember if you hire a listing agent, you will pay them plus you will pay the buyer's broker. So if your answer to this question is ultimately *yes*, you are deciding to end your FSBO.

And I am not here to change your mind one way or the other. But I would like to point out something odd about these two phone calls. When brokers call, whether they use scripts or not, their demeanor seems to be one of helpfulness. And if they are really slick, cheerful helpfulness. *Let me help you by bringing you a buyer.* Or *let me help you by listing your property.* But in my experience, if you put forth any hesitation or resistance, especially if you make it clear you are not putting up with any scripted nonsense, you can easily detect a sense of...*entitlement*. Yes, I think that is the best word for it.

Yes, amazingly, there's often an edge to these conversations. Entitlement to what? Payment. With an undercurrent of: If you don't recognize that you need me and agree to pay me, clearly you're a fool. Now I know many sellers never pickup on this. But just listen for it. If it is not there, maybe you are talking to a competent broker who does not need to play games. But if you do detect this underlying attitude, move on quickly.

Let me stop here for a question: Why don't these brokers turn their payment entitlement attitude towards their own clients, the buyer? I am not sure, but it may be because, in order to acquire the buyer as a client, they told the buyer that they are paid by the seller. Right?

Now, this is a book on competence: Most listing solicitation phone calls will not come from competent brokers. This is clearly a *Client Acquisition* activity. So most phone calls will come from brokers who focus on that side of the business. As for the first type of phone call, most competent brokers will not care if you are paying them or not. If you are paying them, great. If not, they will include it in the offer. They know it is all about the net. Point is, competent brokers are much less likely to ask about payment. So when they call you, the question is simply: *Hey can we come see it?* Listen for the difference.

Finally, there is a third phone call: *Hey my wife and I saw your house online, can we come see it?* And this is call number three, because like I said, most buyer's have brokers. Now, your response should be a question: *Yes absolutely, do you have a broker?* Because you want to know, and sometimes they have been told not to tell you. In any case, just because they have a broker, at this point you have not agreed and are not obligated to pay their broker. If they do, sooner or later, you will have conversation one from above.

But if the buyer does not have a broker, there is sometimes (perhaps often) a whole new set of challenges. If they like your house and want to move forward, what do you and the buyer do next?

Now I assure you, the point of this longish chapter has not been to end by saying you need to hire a broker. But if you FSBO, you do need to be prepared for what to do next.

The good news is there are solutions. Both parties want pricing help, on what to offer and what to accept. Get an appraisal. Or both sides can get their own appraisal. The buyer likely does not have a written offer. Tell the buyer to go hire an attorney (they will have to anyway) and give them some level of comfort that you will wait. Because it does take some time and they will be spending money on this.

Again, returning to the top of this chapter: The reason you hire a broker is not because you cannot do it. Rather, the reason you hire a broker is to save yourself time. The time to do it, but also, the greater amount of time spent learning how to do it.

Nevertheless, there's never been a better time to FSBO. And if you believe my previous chapter, it is going to get even better.

Section Four:

Marketing

Chapter 32: Marketing is a Commodity

There are any number of things that a broker can do to market your property. But for most properties, the basics will get the job done. Price and presentation including excellent photos and floor plans, a MLS listing with internet syndication (to Zillow and other sites), an attractive, noticeable yard sign with flyers, accessibility to the property. Beyond the basics, anything else is fine. Just don't pay extra for them, no matter how eloquent the broker's *Marketing Plan*.

I will let you in on a little secret: Assuming you hire a minimally competent broker, these marketing basics are commodities and should be priced as such. Sure, some brokers are worth more than others. But the price differential should not be based on anything other than transactional competence. Any idiot can add your property to the MLS; a savvy real estate negotiator is something else entirely.

~~~

I want to tell you what absolutely no one else will: Residential real estate marketing is a commodity endeavor.

Yes, heresy! My marketing professor would be appalled.

Let's start with an example of two brokers:

The first broker does only the basics described above. And no more. But let's talk about those basics for a second: They must be competently executed. The price must be correct [13] and the presentation must be excellent, the photos are the most important marketing asset and must also be excellent, floor plans and feature sheets have become standard, the

---

[13] But I do not mean underpriced. I mean *correct* as we have discussed it.

property must be properly syndicated so that it shows up everywhere on the internet. Even in 2020, attractive yard signs with informative flyers are still important. And brokers must have a discussion with sellers about making sure buyers have access to the property without difficulty. Okay, you get the *basic* idea.

Now the second broker comes in with the most beautiful *Marketing Plan* you've ever seen. Printed on crisp fifty-pound, richly-colored paper to leave with you as a keepsake. Then, he whips out his iPad to go through it all with you PowerPoint-style. Naturally it includes the basics above. But he sniffs: *I go above and beyond.* He advertises on radio and television, he has a billboard on the highway. He'll have open houses and broker open houses. His firm is part of a pricey national franchise that will send him buyer leads, he pays Zillow for additional leads, and he pays relocation companies for even more leads. He sends out mailings and pays for an email marketing service, his office is in an expensive retail center, he pays for a *talking house* service, and individual property websites, and a moving van for buyer and sellers. And he pays a motivational sales coach to keep himself in the *right* frame of mind, and he leases an expensive car to make the *right* impression. He makes a dozen phone calls a day looking for buyers for each listing. Look, the list could be endless.

Now this extra stuff is great and all, and certainly cannot hurt, but make no mistake about it, it is not designed to sell your house. The basics will be more than adequate for 99% of all houses. So what is all this extra stuff and elaborate *Marketing Plan* really about? Well two things.

First, it is simply designed to acquire the seller as a client. *Mr. Seller, look at everything I am going to do for you*. But it is not about *conveying real property* because much of this stuff is nonsense. It is entirely about *client acquisition*. That is, putting on a dog-and-pony show for the seller. I mean look at this stuff: Email marketing campaigns? Mailings? Talking houses? Phone calls? Franchises and expensive offices in an internet age? Surely they're kidding? And none of it is going to sway a buyer one way or the other. No, buyers will only buy the right house for them, no matter what. The real purpose of all this crap is to acquire the seller as a client.

And second, while this stuff may not help market the seller's house, much of it will help market the broker, himself, and help him secure more clients. So what the broker is really doing is marketing himself, to other potential clients, on the seller's dime.

I just have to say that again: *Brokers market themselves on the seller's dime*.

Now some will say: But surely everything that can be done to attract buyers, should be done. Well guess what? Serious home buyers are not passive. Buyers are not sitting around waiting for you to reach out to them: Hey, buy my house! No, serious buyers are actively searching for the right home. So what sellers need to do is to make sure that those buyers can find them. Do more if you like, but you are wasting your time, effort, and money. And probably doing more for your broker than for yourself.

Now let's ask: Is there such a thing as a passive home buyer? You know someone not really looking to move, but might possibly be convinced, if they were informed about your house being for sale? Well brokers would have you believe this is the bulk of the buyer pool. And they want to convince you that this is where they need to focus their marketing, and this is why all this elaborate marketing and expense is necessary. But to the extent that brokers do reach these people, the broker is not asking them to buy your home. The odds there are simply too long. No, the broker is hoping to also acquire them as clients, either as buyers or sellers. It has nothing to do with the seller or the seller's house.

So, is it possible that a passive home buyer will make an offer on your house? Sure. But what are the odds? My position is: Let's spend our limited resources on those most likely to buy your house: Actively searching buyers. Overwhelmingly so. Let's put the question another way. What is more likely: That a seller locates the right buyer, or that a buyer locates the right house?

Let's not allow ourselves to be distracted by a bunch of nonsense here. The way these brokers market, both houses and themselves, is dishonest and contemptible. Don't fall for it.

So let's continue with the basics: Surely not all marketing basics are the same? Surely, some brokers are better marketers than other brokers, and some marketing is better than other marketing? Right?

Clearly so. But with a minimal level of competence, the results are the same. Do some real estate brokers write better copy than others? Absolutely. Does it matter? Probably not.

Let's take another example: Two houses for sale in the same neighborhood. One has the most beautiful ad copy that you have ever seen, in the MLS listing and on the expensively-printed marketing flyer, full color, high gloss, artistic photos from a bespoke photographer, and a three-dimensional floor plan. The other has minimally competent copy, black-and-white flyers printed on plain copy paper, rather journeyman-like photos, and a two-dimensional floor plan. You get the distinction.

Which house gets seen the most? Which house gets sold fastest and for the most money? Well if all else is equal, we don't have enough information to answer these questions.

Notice, I did not ask, which house gets seen first? Because yes, maybe the best marketing will lead buyers to come see that house first. But guess what? They are going to see the other house as well. Every single time. And which of the two will they buy? The one that meets their needs and desires. And that may or may not be the one with the best marketing. We'll come to this in the next chapter.

But for now, my fellow real estate brokers will argue: But the goal is to get buyers to come see this house first and make an offer before seeing anything else. And then my question to these brokers becomes: Oh really…how stupid do you think buyers are? Even if they leave the first house to go write an offer on it, the buyers are going to stop at the second house, for a quick look, on the way out of the neighborhood. But brokers do not think enough of buyers or sellers to even acknowledge this. Again, it's a lack of respect.

Look, I am not saying that marketing is not important. The difference here is not between marketing and no marketing. Rather it is between the absolute best and most elaborate and most expensive marketing and perfectly sufficient marketing. Between one broker's beautifully-written and elaborate *Marketing Plan* and another broker who simply, but competently, executes the basics.

Because for most residential properties, the basics are more than enough. If you have a million-dollar villa on a mountaintop, those buyers are few and far between, and perhaps you need the best marketing money can buy. But if you have our typical $500,000 house in our typical $500,000 neighborhood, you need the basics.

Now why is this important? If a broker offers more marketing or the best marketing, why would a seller not take it? It certainly cannot hurt. The answer is: Because brokers are using the illusion of over-the-top marketing to first acquire the seller as a client, and then as an excuse to charge that seller top dollar. Hire me, and pay me six percent, because my marketing is second to none.

But you do not need *second to none* marketing. So don't pay for it. Much of it does not work anyway, much of it just helps the broker, and none of it will sway a buyer.

One final point: Remember at the top of this chapter, I said: assuming you hire a *minimally competent* broker. So I am not saying that incompetent marketing is sufficient. The photos cannot be bad (and we've all seen bad real estate photos). The curb appeal and presentation must be sufficiently attractive. The ad copy must be more than merely articulate. I would go so far as to say that, of course, the basic marketing must be excellent. Competent. Just don't overpay for it and don't allow a broker to use marketing basics or extras to justify their inflated fee.

Because all competent brokers will do the basics, sure with some variations, the basics are commodities and should be priced as such. Don't pay for more.

Chapter 33: Marketing Will Not Sell Your House

No amount of marketing will sell your house. The goal of real estate marketing is to alert actively searching buyers that your house is available for sale, that it may fit their needs and desires, and to get them to come take a look at it. Then the house itself will either meet their needs and desires, or it will not. Don't pretend otherwise. Any marketing that stretches beyond this goal is a waste of time, effort, and money.

~~~

The goal of marketing is to get buyers in the door. It can do no more. What sells a house, the only thing that sells a house, is the question:

Does the house meet the needs and desires of the buyer?

Will a lower price open up the buyer pool? Absolutely. Will fresh neutral paint in the photos draw more people? Sure. Is price a buyer need and/or desire? Most often. Can a buyer desire a home that is *move-in ready*? Absolutely. But the buyer can have any number of needs and desires, and the seller can only guess what they are or might be.

Let me give you a not uncommon example using neutral color. I have seen more than one buyer take possession of a house, a freshly painted in a neutral color house, and immediately repaint it in yet a different neutral color.

I think as a rule, it is healthy and just good business practice to have a certain level of respect for the buyer. It is important, even vital, to consider residential real estate from the perspective of the buyer's needs and desires.

What does this mean? This means that the goal of marketing, the basics and even the unnecessary extras, is to simply alert actively searching buyers that the house is available for sale, that it may fit their needs and desires, and to get them to come take a look at it.

And if the property meets their needs and desires, they will make an offer. If it does not quite meet their needs and desires, but it is the best fit given the alternatives, they might still make an offer. If there is a better alternative, they will not make an offer at all. And there is nothing a seller can do about that except wait for another buyer.

Don't forget, the seller certainly has no control over those alternatives. The seller only controls two things: One, are the buyers able to discover that the house is for sale? And two, the price and presentation of the house, along with any changes in these they might be willing to make. That's it.

Now, do buyers ever buy houses for other reasons? It would be naive to say *no*. Let's make up an example: The wife of the buyer's boss is a real estate broker, and she has a listing that is close to what the buyer is looking for. Maybe the buyer will buy that over a better alternative. Maybe. But even here, is that not really meeting a desire of the buyer? In this case, the desire to please or appease his boss. But for the most part, this is such a large expense, that the buyer's actual needs and desires will be paramount.

Okay I hear you: This is obvious and redundant; why are we talking about this?

Because so many real estate brokers think of themselves as sales people. They did not get the memo, back in Chapter One, that *conveying real property* is not a sales job, but rather it is a customer service job. Or perhaps more likely, they are so wrapped up in the sales aspect of *client acquisition* that they don't even understand the two primary jobs.

And don't get me wrong, I do not care what brokers think or how they think of themselves or even if they think at all. But don't let them tell you that they, or their marketing prowess, will sell your house. Don't let them convince you that it is worthwhile to pay more for marketing that stretches beyond this stated goal. Besides, odds are, that such marketing does more for the broker than it does to, you know, sell the house.

Now if you put this chapter in front of them, they will slickly explain that the writer is indeed the naive one because everyone knows that real estate is a sales job. So don't kid yourself Mr. Seller; like it or not, you need a salesperson. *It's a sales job you idiot*.

But dear reader, let me ask you: Did anyone *sell* you your current home? See, I think the answer is *no*. Because otherwise you would not be reading this book. And even if the answer is *yes*, I think you are reading this book because you now know that was a mistake.

Isn't it time that we all got serious?

The Basics of Online Marketing

I once represented a professional copy editor as his listing broker. Of course I handled it like any other house. But when I presented him with my listing materials, he asked if he could write his own copy. Right? I mean, of course he did. And me, hey I am a journeyman copywriter at best. And I thought, well now, I am about to learn how it's done. Right? Of course I did.

Now luckily for this story, and I am not making this up, this was your typical $500,000 house in your typical $500,000 neighborhood.

So when I receive his revised copy, I was rather surprised to discover that he had basically moved some of my words and sentences around, and then sent it back to me. There was certainly nothing new, or in my opinion, even improved. Now this is a highly educated and highly paid professional. Why was this the case? I mean, how was this even possible?

Well if he had been given unlimited marketing and copywriting space, I have no doubt that he would have blown me away. We see this sort of thing with high-end homes, say over a million dollars. But these days, I am not even sure that number is high enough.

Let me give you an extreme example. If you are selling a multi-million-dollar villa on top of a mountain, in Tuscany, you may well need to produce an elaborate marketing campaign which would certainly include a twelve-page, full-color glossy brochure, with lots of room for bespoke photography and the most creative copy imaginable. And you would put together a high-end, colorful website with even more room for copy and unlimited photos and video. You would have video walk throughs and drone photography and dramatic night time photography. Here your marketing is designed to appeal to an elite, but very small and hard to reach, audience. And just think of the cost.

But if you are selling a typical $500,000 house in a typical $500,000 neighborhood, you want your marketing to reach a much broader audience. Now you could put together a similar brochure and website, and it would certainly not hurt. But let's just ask the question: How are ninety-nine potential buyers out of a hundred going to find your house? Well they are not going to visit the special online real estate advertising supplement of *The Wall Street Journal,* to find an expensive ad for your house with a website, and request the expensively-produced brochure. They are just not.

No, they are going to Zillow and other similar sites. And they may rely on their buyer's broker to search the local MLS for them (by the way, brokers automate these searches).

Today most MLS systems have the ability to syndicate listings to other sites like Zillow and Trulia and Realtor.com, etc. The MLS also sends the data to each MLS member broker to use on their own websites. So the broker and the buyer are basically seeing the same available properties. The broker can send them what is available in the MLS which is a bit more than the syndicated data. But the available properties are the same.

What is important to note here is that the MLS, as a computer system, has limits on how much data (text and photos) that it will accept. And certainly the syndication process has data limits as well. And these amounts are relatively small.

It should also be noted that in recent years, MLS systems have added the ability to add documents to listings. Brokers will upload surveys, floor plans, disclosure statements, HOA documents, feature sheets, etc. into the MLS system. If a broker or a graphic designer creates a property brochure, the broker can add it to the listing as well (at least as a low-resolution document). But these documents are not syndicated and are therefore only accessible by member brokers.

For syndication, you only get so much text space and a finite number of photos. So basic marketing must fit into this system with its data constraints. Believe it or not, even in 2020, these data spaces are limited to a given number of characters (not words, characters). So brokers must choose each word for maximum impact.

You can describe the master bathroom as a: *Spacious self-indulgent oasis tucked away from the bustle of everyday life.* Or you can simply describe it as a: *Large master bath*, because you want to save room to also mention the oversized three-car garage. So you can see how this leads to rather efficient but prosaic copy. This is why my copy editor client (and hopefully still friend) was not really able to improve my copy of admittedly limited skill.

Now sure, you can do more. Brokers can do as much or as little as they like. So yes, brokers can and do set up a websites that offer loads of additional marketing material on each of their properties. With an unlimited number of photos and video and the most creative copy imaginable. With video walk throughs and drone photography and dramatic night time photography. And of course, the downloadable twelve-page, full-color brochure (in high resolution). Sound familiar? But mostly what you find is some subset of this. Sometimes more, most often less. In any case, whatever is done and however much is done, is helpful. Right?

Well…let's not forget to ask the elementary marketing questions: Who is my target market and how are they going to find me? And what is our goal?

As we discussed, the goal is to simply alert actively searching buyers that the house is available for sale, that it may fit their needs and desires, and to get them to come take a look at it. With that in mind, what we need to do with real estate marketing is balance cost and reach. For most properties, we need to reach a broad audience without spending a fortune. And the MLS/syndication system, even with all of its limitations, offers a very efficient way to do just that.

That individual broker website? Not so much. Because even if it shows up in a Google search, or even if the broker pays Google to have it show up at the very top of the search results, that is not how the overwhelming number of buyers are searching for houses. No, regardless of what website the buyer is using, he or she is searching the syndicated data. Because that is the most efficient way for any buyer to see all the available houses. Not to see the *most* houses available; rather to see *all* the houses.

The idea that a buyer will visit all, or even multiple, broker websites to search for houses is fallacious. It is just not a very efficient way for an actively searching buyer to go about it. No, they are going to find a website they like to use, or maybe two or three, and search there – Seeing the syndicated data. And/or they can have their broker send them the greater amount of data out of the MLS system directly.

In either case, buyers are most often not searching broker website to broker website. I am not saying it does not happen. But even if a buyer searches this way, the vast amount of what they are finding and viewing is syndicated data. So the questions are: How many buyers are doing that? Is it worth the expense? And will we not reach our goal of getting them in the door without the additional expense?

Real estate brokers produce a lot of online noise. And today, any Google real estate search has a lot of noise. Really too much noise to be useful. On the other hand, syndication offers results searchable by buyer-selected parameters in buyer-selected locales. These websites immediately present the buyer with exactly what he or she is looking for.

Let me go further and make what I believe you will find to be a rather surprising claim: For a broker to effectively market properties online, it is absolutely not necessary to have any separate online presence for the property itself or even for the broker himself.

Let me say that again: A broker does not need an internet presence, at all. The MLS/syndication system, alone, is more than adequate. His listings show up on all other broker websites with a search function. Here I mean the large brokerage firms that maintain fancy websites with search functions. And I mean, the individual broker websites that offer very little, but almost always include a search function as well. And, on the non-broker websites like Zillow. Our broker may not have a web presence, but his listings are plastered all over the internet. Isn't that the online marketing goal?

Hawking a villa in Tuscany, maybe a website is required (although you are probably not going to rely on Google).

Hawking a property under a million dollars in Austin, Texas? Not so much.

Here is the point: Brokers design these websites to impress sellers, not find buyers. So the broker's website and individual property websites are often just another part of the broker's dog-and-pony show to acquire the seller as a client. Oh, and to justify their fees.

One more point before we will leave this. Are there passive buyers viewing the MLS/syndicated listings? You bet. I have no idea how many, but a lot of people enjoy window shopping real estate. But as for actively searching buyers, and there can be no doubt about this: They are all here.

Finally, if a broker lists your property as *Coming Soon*, and puts it solely on his own website, the property is of course, not syndicated. The whole goal of coming soon is that the broker is attempting to acquire the buyer as a client in a dual agency situation. So they have no incentive to *share* the listing anywhere. They want potential buyers to come to their website and browse their coming soon listings. So instead of showing up across the internet, the house only shows up on the broker's website. So not only is coming soon designed to lead to dual agency, it is also a huge disservice to the sellers in terms of marketing reach and breadth. I have doubts as to whether or not this is properly explained to sellers.

It should be noted that as of this writing our local MLS is changing the rules to force brokers to syndicate Coming Soon listings to other member brokers. But still not to non-broker websites like Zillow and others. This is certainly a step in the right direction. Hopefully this will lessen the incentives for this shady practice. Time will tell.

Chapter 34: Open Houses are a Sham

I question the efficacy of open houses. But every time I express my skepticism, someone always reports a positive result. So let me put the question this way: If a potential buyer attends an open house, and is serious enough to subsequently make an offer, would that same potential buyer not have been willing to make an appointment to see the house? With his own broker, on his own schedule. It seems to me that the only reason to have an open house is to convert tire kickers into offer-writers. I am not saying that it cannot happen, but what are the odds?

So why do brokers hold open houses? Well it has very little to do with selling your house. Rather, brokers see an open house as an opportunity to pick up buyers as the broker on the buy side. Personally, I find the whole enterprise to be a bit of a sham. When holding an open house, a broker misleads the seller as to his true intentions and thereby falsely raises the hopes of the seller. And at the same time, the broker is meeting potential buyers (for other properties) under false pretenses.

~~~

I'm sorry, but open houses are not an activity designed to *convey real property*. Rather they are full square in the middle of the *client acquisition* side of the business. The broker knows that it is extremely unlikely that a potential buyer, who shows up at an open house, will ultimately make an offer on that house. But by golly, the broker wants to hold your house open at least once every weekend until it sells. I have even seen brokers hold open houses after a contract is in place, looking, supposedly, for a backup offer.

Why? Well, it may be unlikely that those potential buyers will make an offer on that particular house, but there's a good chance they will make an offer on some house. And if these buyers are attending an open house, they probably do not yet have their own broker. So yes, the broker sees an open house as an opportunity to acquire another client.

This might be fine for a vacant property. And I would feel better about open houses if brokers would be honest with their clients as to their true intentions. But think about what an honest broker would have to say: *Hey Mr. Seller, do you mind if I hold an open house in your vacant property, so that maybe I can pickup some buyer clients?* And hey, if the property is vacant, and if the broker has a good relationship with the seller, sure, why not ask? But the idea of asking sellers to leave their occupied home on a Sunday afternoon under false pretenses...well, that's just pretty low.

Wow, it turns out that this is one of the shortest chapters in the book. I am a bit surprised. But honestly, I just have nothing else to say about this topic.

Chapter 35: Buyer Feedback

No honest broker will promise the seller *feedback* from every showing. Yet in order to help secure a listing, some brokers will do just that. They make this promise even though this is not in their control. The problem is that feedback may not be in the buyer's best interest, and so savvy buyers may not provide it. This may or may not be important to you. But it is a great little indicator of how honest a broker is.

Buyers should ask their broker whether or not he is providing *feedback* to the sellers on every showing. It is unfortunate that this is necessary. But many brokers will do this as a matter of course, never even discussing the matter with their client. They do this, supposedly, as a *courtesy* to the seller and the listing broker. Yes, they seem to forget for whom they work. Yet feedback may not be in a buyer's best interest and may even weaken a buyer's negotiating position. Again, this may or may not be important to you. But it is a great little indicator of a broker's integrity and how serious they take their fiduciary responsibilities.

~~~

When a broker goes out on a listing appointment to pitch their services they tell the potential seller client what they will do for the seller and why the seller should become their client. The list of services offered by the broker will vary from firm to firm and from broker to broker. As we have discussed, there may or may not be a correlation between service level and price. But there is one service that costs the broker nothing, and therefore, it is almost always included – no, promised, to potential seller clients: Feedback.

Mr. Seller, if you hire me, I will solicit feedback from any and all potential buyers and their brokers. And, we can use this invaluable information to help market the home.

But feedback is more than this. Often listing brokers will use buyer feedback to help the broker tell the now seller client something the broker does not want to say themselves, or something the seller does not want to hear, or something the broker has, in fact, told the seller, but the seller did not believe. So far, so good. Actually, sounds beneficial – and it is. For the seller and the seller's broker.

But what about the buyer? When they are out viewing properties, are the buyers and their broker taking notes? Well maybe. It depends…on the buyers' reactions, the accuracy of the MLS data, the style of the particular broker and of the particular buyers, etc. If the goal is to narrow the number of properties, it is highly unlikely that they are going to take the time to write notes about choices number four and five. Four and Five are out – really nothing further to discuss – let's move on. Or, let's go write an offer on Number One. Right?

But in any case, later when the buyer's broker gets a chance to check her email, what does he find? Well, an inbox full of Feedback Requests. Now most real estate brokers want to be well-liked by their peers. So brokers will sit down and accommodate these requests.

Yessiree, they will sit right there and say things like, *My buyers did not like the wallpaper in the hall bath*, or *We thought that the factory right behind the house was a wee bit loud*, or even, *Gosh, the price seemed a little high to us, but thank you ever so much for letting us see it*. Or, they might say: *Golly gee wiz, my clients just loved the place*.

They might even say: *My clients just loved the place and it is in right zone for the school where they want to send their kids.* This actually happened to us once. And when we looked it up, the house was the only one for sale in that zone. Give that some thought. No really, give that some thought.

Believe it or not, this is standard operating procedure for most buyer's brokers. I often wonder: Is it also standard operating procedure to inform their buyers of this practice?

Here I would like to propose the *Savvy Buyer Feedback Maxim*:

> The more a buyer likes a property, the more likely honest feedback will only serve to hurt his interests.
>
> Corollary: The less a buyer likes a property, the less the buyer and his broker found noteworthy (good or bad).

Now, I wish this was the end of the story, but it's not….

I typically do not provide feedback. The only way I will do so is when I am beyond certain that my buyer client has zero interest in a property AND I have the time and inclination to do a *favor* for the listing broker (yes, this does happen). Plus, I do have to remember the place, right?

But in my experience, if and when a broker fails to respond to the first email Feedback Request, yes, they will get another, and then another. And low and behold, if all those emails fail to do the trick, the listing broker, or one of his minions, starts calling. Yes, on the phone. After all, he *promised* his seller clients feedback. And, usually it is the broker from un-noteworthy choice number five, and usually this is two or three days later, and always when I am in the middle of something terribly important. And, they say, do you remember my listing….?

The conversation goes downhill from there….

Chapter 36: On Pricing Real Estate Like Groceries

Another question: Do you really believe that $499,900 is a better and smarter price than $500,000? Someone who can afford to purchase your property is not going to be swayed by such nonsense. Why insult them?

~~~

Evidently some time ago, some researcher, somewhere, maybe an academic, maybe he worked for Del Monte or Kellogg's, came up with the bright idea that consumers are more likely to pickup a $0.99 can of green beans over a $1.00 can of green beans.

Right?

And ever since then, American consumers have come to expect this nonsense, even if it is just a bit insulting. And of course we see this style of pricing for all consumer goods, clothing, white goods, furniture, automobiles, lot's of things… the pricing of dry cleaning. Certainly we all see this with gasoline.

But here's my question: How long ago were these studies done? Fifty years ago? Longer? Would I be wrong to make the proposition that American consumers are much wiser today than they were when this practice became the standard? Yet it continues. I think, not really out of a question of *what works*, but rather, out of *habit*.

Personally, I think it is a bad habit. But I might be convinced to accept it if I could be convinced that it works. Don't take my opinion on this. Answer the question for yourself: Are you more likely to pick up a $0.99 can of green beans that you don't really like or a $1.00 can that you prefer?

See, at least today, it is not about the perception of price; we all know the price is the same. So, what do we do? We pickup the beans that we prefer.

Maybe canned goods are not the best example: You are considering two sofas at two different stores. One is $999 and the other is $1,000. Do you really believe that anyone would buy the $999 sofa over the $1,000 sofa if they happen to prefer (for whatever reason) the $1,000 sofa? Again, it is not about price perception. Today it is about preference.[14]

So I would like to make the following proposition: With real estate, it is today, and it has always been, about preference. This odd pricing nonsense never sold any real estate. The price point is too high, and the decision is too important, for a buyer to be swayed by this claptrap. For real estate, this pricing method is specious; it is silly and adolescent. And if it had ever been effective, I would call it out-of-date.

And yet, we see this all the time in real estate pricing. It is, I think, testament to the inability or unwillingness of real estate brokers to think for themselves. The term intellectually vacant comes to mind, but I am not sure they would get the pun.

In fact, there are some studies that suggest odd pricing in the other direction (e.g. $501,534) leads, on average, to a

---

[14] In fact, *odd pricing* dates back over one hundred years. Conventional wisdom and numerous studies say it works because people read left to right. Therefore, the left-most figure is the most important in terms of perception. So the real question is: Today, does perception outweigh preference? You judge for yourself. My personal opinion is that odd pricing worked when there was less selection and therefore less comparison shopping. Clearly different from today. I also believe that this perception business diminishes with each additional digit and by the time you get to, say, six-figures, it is practically nonexistent. Six figures, as in the price of a house.

higher negotiated final *Purchase Price* for the seller.[15] But if one wants a higher negotiated final *Purchase Price*, instead of playing games like this, it might be more productive to focus on one's negotiating skills. I don't think it is a stretch to suggest that most Americans, including most real estate brokers, could benefit from improvement in this skill set.

But there is something else.

Could we return to our typical $500,000 house. Specifically, could we consider the buyers for such a house. We have already discussed that buyers are finding their own houses, and we've also discussed the fact that they are doing so online.

But specifically, how do $500,000-buyers go about searching for a $500,000 house? It's not a trick question. They pull up a real estate website and enter search terms. Right? Here's something they don't do: They don't simply enter $500,000. As in show me all the $500,000 properties. No of course not; they enter a range. Say for example, $475,000 to $525,000. Right?

And really, there will be buyers who enter: $450,000 to $500,000. Right? And others, who will enter $500,000 to $535,000. Right? So that makes three possibilities: The figure may be at the top, or at the bottom, or somewhere in the middle.

I might add, in passing, notice all the zeros. No one searches for $474,999 to $524,900.

---

[15] As an example, see Eric Cardella and Michael Seiler, *The effect of listing price strategy on real estate negotiations*, Journal of Economic Psychology. 23 November 2015.

But there is something else I want you to notice. If you price your home at $499,900, it does not show up in the search range of $500,000 to $525,000. Nope, it is not there. Even if it is *the* perfect match for the buyer.

Alternatively, if you price your home at $500,000 it shows up in all three search possibilities.

So even if you do not agree with my opinion on odd pricing foolishness, here is a practical reason for even pricing: Let's get the property in front of the greatest number of buyers.

I would even go so far as to say: The more zeros, the better.

Section Five:

Negotiation

Chapter 37: The Negotiating Platform

Understand that residential real estate negotiating is different from most other negotiations. Whether the parties use the actual standard contract form or not, it is the platform on which the negotiation takes place.

And regardless of how the negotiation takes place, once the parties reach an agreement, they will reduce it to writing, almost always using the standard form. Therefore, for each party, a favorably executed contract form is the negotiating goal. So advanced knowledge and understanding of this form contract is a tremendous advantage.

~~~

In North Carolina, the state association of REALTORS® and the state bar jointly operate a Forms Committee to create and update various forms used by buyers and sellers of real property in the state. The most important form they maintain is the *Offer to Purchase and Contract*. Buyers will typically use this form to make an offer. Then the seller may use the same form to make any counter-offer. And finally, when and if the two sides come to an agreement, both sign, and the same form becomes a contract.

I should point out, that in our state, as of this writing, this form is fourteen pages long. It seems to grow a page every two or three years as the committee makes annual adjustments and updates to reflect ever changing market conditions. The point is, it includes many terms, beyond the *Purchase Price*, all of which the parties can negotiate.

It is also important to note that, use of this form is not required; buyers and sellers of real property are legally able to create their own offer and contract. So for example, many builders will use their own contracts. These are most often written by the builder's attorney, and needless to say, favor the builder. And for commercial property, buyers and sellers will often use unique, attorney-drafted instruments. This is fine, but it is not cheap, and it is not immediate.

So there are several benefits of the form offer and contract for residential real estate. One, the form is party neutral, so both sides are comfortable using it. Two, it is standard, so buyers and sellers, do not need an attorney to draft a unique document each and every time they need to convey property. Three, therefore it is cheap to use and immediately available.

So for re-sale (non-new-construction), in 99 transactions out of 100, this is the form that the buyers and sellers use to document the agreement. Even if there is some non-standard item that the parties want to address in the contract, most often they still use the form and add an addendum.

Does any other business work like this? I mean, at least on such a large scale? Take our cousins on the commercial side of the business. Yes, they have similar forms available, which the parties often use for straightforward deals. But for transactions with any complexity, the parties will typically use the unique, attorney-drafted documents I mentioned.

So the negotiations for those deals are more open-ended. They start, not with a form, but literally with a blank sheet of paper. The parties negotiate and agree on terms, write them down on this blank sheet of paper, and label it a *Letter of Intent*. Then the attorney uses this to produce the unique contract.

Think about it, in most other substantive business negotiations, something similar takes place. And the result is the perfect instrument for the deal as conceived by the parties. But it is also expensive and time-consuming.

Too expensive and time-consuming for most residential real estate deals. So we have this very unique and peculiar negotiation process based on the *Offer to Purchase and Contract*. This form is the negotiating platform. Okay, okay, this is straightforward enough; why go on about it?

Command the platform, command the deal.

I don't mean command as in *order* or *to give an order*. Rather, I mean knowledge and mastery. Perhaps it would be better put this way: Command of the platform is more likely to lead to command of the deal. You get the point.

As designed, the buyer will complete the form as he would like the contract to read, and send it along to the seller, who will then make and initial changes, as he would like the contract to read. And this goes back and forth until the two parties reach an agreement. Then both sign, and presto, we have a contract.

Now sure, that works, and we see that, not infrequently. But after the buyer sends the initial written offer, often times the next stages of back and forth happen on the phone. And the telephone conversations do not address each blank on all fourteen pages. Rather, the parties or their brokers, discuss the *open* items, where the two parties have yet to reach agreement. And there is a certain fluidity to this process, because as the parties reach agreement on one item, this may affect others. Think: *We'll give you this, but we will then want that*.

Now if the buyer originally sent a written form offer, the two parties are typically referring to that document to have these telephone conversations. Right? Of course. The same is true if the back and forth happens via email. So whether the actual form goes back and forth with each iteration, it is the form that the parties are using to begin, narrow, and complete the negotiation process.

But that need not be true. In order to save time, savvy buyers may simply call or email with proposed terms. With no form in sight. Think: *Will you take X price?* Now it is usually the price and other major terms, other monies, dates, etc. But clearly, not fourteen pages of items, because then they would have simply used the form. Of course, the seller can add any term that he wants. If the buyer did not include a term, because perhaps it was not important to him, but it is important to the seller, be assured, the seller will add it to the back and forth, however that takes place.

But even here, these terms are all, generally found in the standard form. And as they are discussed and negotiated, a broker does so with the form in mind. He asks himself: How will I complete the form to accomplish that desired, or later agreed, item? And less often he might think: The form has no allowance for this desired item, and therefore, we will need something beyond the form. This thought process may go on in his head. Or, he might actually refer to a blank form.

Like I said at the top of this chapter, whether the parties use the actual form, or not, it is in fact the platform on which the negotiation takes place. Because sooner or later, the parties will complete that form to record their agreement.

So the standard form is the primary tool of the real estate negotiation process. And the more command you have over this tool, the more likely you are to achieve your goals or the goals of your principal.

Now sadly, it is not a simple form. And frankly, how it works is not immediately obvious. I think I can say without exaggeration, that most people, reading the form once or twice, will not understand it or the transactional effects of it.

So read it, think about, read it again, etc. Practice using it. Or…find someone who has.

As an aside: I hope you will agree with me, that my chapter on FSBOs was fairly supportive of sellers who wish to go down this route. But now let me point out where they often fail: They do not take the time to understand the contract, or get help understanding the contract. And as I put at the top of that chapter: Brokers and savvy buyers take advantage of their hubris. Yes I know, you thought I forgot.

Finally, this is not a book about any particular real estate contract. Each state form is different, and one would have to write fifty books. But before we leave the real estate contract completely, in our next chapter we will discuss the most important contractual element in terms of the negotiating process: Due Diligence.

Compctont negotiation begins with command of your state's standard form real estate contract.

Chapter 38: Negotiating Due Diligence

A complete understanding of the Due Diligence provisions of the standard *Offer to Purchase and Contract* is a huge negotiating advantage. Use it. Even if they have read it, most people, including many real estate brokers, do not understand it.

~~~

Today, many states use a standard form offer and contract which includes some type of due diligence provisions. The simplest way I know to describe this is to say that the contract, when fully executed is an option to purchase contract. The standard form contract grants the buyer an option to purchase the property with the contractually agreed-upon terms, for some negotiated period of time. During this period, the buyer can decide if he wants to move forward with the purchase, or not.

In return for this option, the buyer pays the seller a nonrefundable option fee, most often labeled the *Due Diligence Fee*. And the time period for making this decision is labeled the *Due Diligence Period*. If during this period, the buyer decides to terminate the contract (typically for any reason or no reason), the seller keeps the fee. And if the buyer does not terminate and therefore moves forward with the transaction, the fee is applied to the *Purchase Price*.

I would argue that other than the *Purchase Price* itself, this option fee, the *Due Diligence Fee*, is the most important term in the offer and contract. I might even go so far as to say, because everything is subject to re-negotiation during the *Due Diligence Period*, including the *Purchase Price*, that actually, the *Due Diligence Fee* is even more important that the *Purchase Price* itself.

While the parties may agree to change any other term of the contract, and while the *Due Diligence Fee* is sometimes increased (say for example if the buyer is asking for more time for his *Due Diligence Period* or more time to close), I have never seen an instance where the *Due Diligence Fee* is reduced. Why? Well, this fee is not escrowed; it is paid directly to the seller. There's no point in reducing it if the transaction moves forward because it applies to *Purchase Price*. And if the transaction is halted for any reason, there's not much chance the seller will give it, or some of it, back to the buyer. So as a practical matter, this figure can only go up.

Point is, pay the *Due Diligence Fee* to the seller…and it is gone. And this is exactly where people, including many real estate brokers, lose the plot. Both sides, buyer and seller, should ask themselves: What are the ramifications of this nonrefundable payment? And the answer to that question is, mostly, a function of how much the payment is. Exactly how much money did the buyer give the seller? Or in the negotiation itself, how much money is the buyer proposing to give the seller?

Because the amount paid determines who controls the transaction. Stop and think about that. If the buyer and seller negotiate some small amount, the buyer has very little to lose by terminating the contract, and therefore the buyer is in control. If the buyer and seller negotiate some large amount, the buyer has a lot to lose by terminating the contract, perhaps even more than he can afford to lose, and therefore the seller is in control.

Now we'll stop here and ask: Surely there is some amount that can be negotiated which would equalize the parties transactional control? And the answer is clearly yes, there is, in theory. But it is difficult to know that figure ahead of time. And of course, a party knows his number, but not the other side's. And because so few people understand the previous paragraph, they end up accepting the wrong amount. Or an amount which later fails to protect their interests. As buyers, they pay too much; as sellers, they accept too little.

The consequences can be grave. The buyer may find many expensive and necessary repairs that need to be made, and of course, ask the seller to make them. But if the buyer gave the seller a large *Due Diligence Fee*, which the seller knows or suspects that the buyer will not walk away from, the seller may decline to make any repairs. Nothing requires him to do so except a desire to consummate the transaction. Alternatively, if the seller accepts too little as the *Due Diligence Fee*, the buyer may request these same repairs and say to the seller, either spend money on these expensive repairs, or I will just walk, because I don't have much to lose.

And it is not just repairs. Because the due diligence process most often gives the buyer the right to terminate for any reason or no reason, during the *Due Diligence Period*, the buyer can re-open any terms for re-negotiation. And worse still, the buyer can inject new terms into the transaction. Yes, out of thin air. Remember, the contract grants the buyer a unilateral right to terminate; the seller enjoys no such privilege. While the seller can refuse any new or altered terms, he does so at the risk that the buyer may exercise his right to terminate. So in their desire to move forward with the transaction, many sellers will ultimately accede to the buyer's new or additional terms.

Is this fair? I know, what a question, right? But indulge me: Is it fair that the buyer has the ability to, basically, re-negotiate the whole deal, and if the seller does not agree to the new terms, the buyer can walk? And, should the buyer not be held somewhat accountable for the terms previously agreed-upon, supposedly in good faith, by both parties? The fact that the buyer can terminate, sometimes means that his original terms were not, in fact, made in good faith. Should the seller have no means of enforcing these terms?

So let me answer this way: The reason a seller would find himself in a position of not being able to enforce the original terms, is that he or his broker failed to properly negotiate the *Due Diligence Fee*. That is to say, the *Due Diligence Fee* is *the enforcement mechanism* available to the seller. And other than simply refusing the new terms, it is the seller's only means of control.

So if a broker tells you that during the *Due Diligence Period* of the contract, *the seller has no control whatsoever* and *the total jeopardy is on the seller*, I assure you, she has failed to properly negotiate the *Due Diligence Fee*. Is it not our job as competent brokers to insure that our clients do not suffer total jeopardy and *are* treated fairly? In fact, as fiduciaries, it is our job to (ethically) represent them to the best of our ability. As an aside, this is so much easier to do when one represents one side or the other, and certainly not both.

Now there are those who argue that the *Due Diligence Fee* should always be a small amount. Their rationale seems to be: The buyer will also be spending money on other due diligence and closing related expenses. So for example, the buyer is also paying for inspections, and paying for an appraisal, and perhaps paying a lender's application fee, and to have the water tested, etc. So the buyer's total out-of-pocket expenses *might* be high, and so the negotiated *Due Diligence Fee* does not need to be very much. Why? Because the actual figure that matters is not the *Due Diligence Fee* itself, but rather the total out-of-pocket expenses of the buyer which include the fee. That total is the real amount the buyer loses if he decides to terminate.

But even if it is the total buyer expenses that matter, this simply becomes part of the due diligence negotiation which will determine control. I would only adjust my advice by saying, sure, when negotiating the *Due Diligence Fee*, you can take into account how much money the buyer *may* spend in addition to the *Due Diligence Fee*. But sometimes the buyers will spend heavily on these items, and sometimes they will not. So this figure is most often unknown, even to the buyer, himself. But I will tell you what is known: The *Due Diligence Fee* itself. My advice: Regardless of which side you are on, negotiate the *Due Diligence Fee* to your fullest advantage paying as little regard to other possible buyer expenses as you can.

Now, how much? How much should you be looking for? Well, if you are the buyer, it is rather straightforward: You want the *Due Diligence Fee* to be as small as possible, and certainly as small as the seller will let you get away with. Personally, I like to start negotiations with a nominal amount. Say $100. If I get asked about it, I refer to the discussion above about all the buyer's other expenses. It is surprising how often this works. But note, for more expensive houses, $500 may well be a nominal amount, right? But it is rare for me to start above $250. Work the other expense argument as much as you can before you begin any real negotiation.

Don't forget, the refundable *Earnest Money* is a separate contract term, and often much more than the *Due Diligence Fee*. Even though it is refundable, this larger figure often helps the buyer get away with a nominal *Due Diligence Fee*. This should not be true, but it is. It should not be true because the *Earnest Money* is completely refundable and the buyer can terminate during the *Due Diligence Period* for any reason or no reason. So essentially, the *Earnest Money* is meaningless. (It is only important in the case of breach after the *Due Diligence Period*). But nevertheless, it is a nice, large, pretty figure, just sitting there. People don't understand this and many brokers don't either, so they allow the *Earnest Money* to make an impact. My advice: Initially, be overly generous with *Earnest Money* to help secure a nominal a *Due Diligence Fee*. If this does not work, you can always back it down as negotiations proceed.

I'll tell you something else that often happens: The seller says, you know, we're gonna need more *Due Diligence* than that (referring to the fee). And representing the buyer, I ask: *Well, okay, what if we double it?* You would also be quite surprised just how often that works. So now we're at $200; still a rather nominal amount. God bless real estate brokers.

Advanced Buyer Tip. Let's say you are in a tight seller's market, and the property you want will undoubtedly receive multiple offers. But you like it a lot, and by golly, you want it no matter what. Besides, you've already lost out on several other properties. Very common in today's market. Bump your *Due Diligence Fee* up to an extreme level, say $5,000. And go ahead an attach your $5,000 check, payable to the seller, to your offer. It's like magic. Even though your offer may not have the highest *Purchase Price*, that's $5,000 directly and immediately into the seller's pocket. *Magic.* Be aware, the seller will make no repairs, and there will be NO further negotiation after contract. If you exercise your right to terminate, you kiss your $5,000 goodbye. But in a tight seller's market, this is often okay with the buyer. You got the house!

So, on the seller's side, how much *Due Diligence Fee* should we be looking for? Well, here it is a little more complicated. Obviously, we are not going to even consider the $100 or $200 figure that *some* brokers will try to get away with. Oh no.

No, the figure must be high enough to *cause pain* [16] to the buyer, if the buyer ultimately decides to walk away from the contract. Ideally, the figure should be an amount that the buyer simply cannot afford to walk away from. And this is often a judgment call, based on the buyer, your house, and the price point. For first time home buyers and starter homes, you know $500 may well be enough, considering their other expenses, to get the job done. Think about it, if they walk away from that $500, they may not have another $500 for the next house they find.

For our typical $500,000 house? That's more difficult. But I can promise you $500, does NOT get the job done. No,

---

[16] Let's define *pain*: In a real estate negotiation and transaction, a financial loss that the counterparts are unable to endure or are unwilling to accept. Or perhaps ultimately do accept, but only after all else fails. *Pain* is a harsh word, and may even be offensive to some who perhaps feel it turns negotiation and business into a blood sport. I appreciate this concern, but use pain only as a technical and financial term.

here you start at four-figures. But it is more of a judgment call.

Now stop: What does: *Getting the job done* mean? For me, it mostly means: If there is any reason that comes up during the *Due Diligence Period*, where the buyer is even just considering termination, that the buyer will promptly stop and reconsider, because the *Due Diligence Fee* is nonrefundable and therefore is (really) a penalty for termination. Or even after the *Due Diligence Period*, it becomes an added penalty for breach. Like I said, the figure must be high enough to cause pain. And clearly this is different for a million dollar home and a one hundred thousand dollar townhouse.

So for example, the buyer asks for a bunch of repairs that the seller does not want to make. As the seller, we want them to accept that not all, or perhaps not any, repairs will be made. That is, without the buyer exercising his right to terminate. Or if the buyer is having a difficult time getting their financing in place. As the seller, we want them to work their lender hard.

So sellers, get as much as you can, regardless of what either broker says (because too often, even the brokers don't understand). But don't try to get so much that the buyer (or his broker) says, you know, I wonder if there is anything wrong with that house? Like I said, it is more of a judgment call.

Now I gave the buyers an advanced tip above. Let me end this longish chapter with a little trick for sellers. You receive an offer with (and I'll just make up some numbers) a $500 *Due Diligence Fee* and $2,000 in *Earnest Money*. Very common. That's a total of $2,500 immediately out of the buyer's pocket. So take a *reasonable* approach and say:

You know, we're quite happy with the $2,500 total and we don't need any more, thank you so much. But could you simply reverse the figures?

My friends, you will be surprised at how often this works. And even if the buyer does not make a complete inversion, they will often come close or close enough to *get the job done*. Why? Because neither they nor their broker understand the ramifications of our modest little request. Now I know, you find that just incredibly difficult to believe. But give it a try.

Optimize the *Due Diligence Fee*, control the transaction.

Negotiating Due Diligence: An Example

We listed a small, older, run-down house, on a highly-desirable parcel. We got at least one offer every day it was listed. After about ten days, we accepted the highest and best offer. Now, because we understood the situation, we had priced the property rather high. And this offer was substantially over our listed price.

Now the North Carolina standard form contract is an "as-is" contract, and during negotiations, we made it clear to all potential buyers, that the sellers would not be making any repairs. This was fine with everyone, because the house was clearly a tear-down and buyers would be purchasing the property for the location of the parcel.

So we go under contract with this high offer. But as is our practice when we represent sellers, we secured a high *Due Diligence Fee*. And when I say *high*, what I mean is, quite a bit higher than is typical in our market. The buyers did want a *Due Diligence Period* for financing purposes, and we had no objection.

But during the *Due Diligence Period*, the buyers had a property inspection and an appraisal. Needless to say, the property did not appraise anywhere near the negotiated *Purchase Price*. The buyers then come back to us and request a price reduction to the appraised value plus a substantial credit for repairs. (Remember, the buyer can ask for anything). At this point their contention is that they have decided to rent out the house for some period of time, before proceeding with their development plans.

With me?

Now let me just ask: When negotiating the original contract, was the buyer acting in good faith? I just don't think they were. I think the buyer never had any intention of fulfilling the terms as originally negotiated. They just wanted the property contracted to themselves knowing they would have an opportunity to get a better deal.

And what recourse does the typical seller have? The buyer thought that we would capitulate to their demands because, if not, we would be forced to disclose all of the material facts (the problems) with the house to any other potential buyers. And of course, these were deal-breakers. The buyers really thought they had us over a barrel.

But we did have multiple interested buyers and multiple offers. And like I said, all buyers had been informed that the sellers would not make repairs. So sure, we disclose all new material facts, but no one cared. Our policy in these situations is to simply turn over the Inspection Report to any other interested buyers. So the sellers were willing to let the buyers terminate, if they so chose, and then sell the property to another buyer.

But what if this had not been the case? What if, these dishonest (bad faith anyway) buyers had submitted the only offer? If we had accepted a nominal amount as a *Due Diligence Fee*, they might very well have gotten away with these shenanigans. *Total jeopardy would have been on the seller,* as our top producer admonished back in Chapter 17.

But these buyers had paid the sellers a substantial *Due Diligence Fee*, which the sellers were keeping regardless. The seller told the buyer, it's the original deal or nothing.

Here the buyers started a gunfight, but they were represented by a rhinestone cowboy completely out of his depth. I use a similar story of a high *Due Diligence Fee* in Chapter 54 on Better Than Expected Offers.

Chapter 39: Try Not to Care (Too Much)

The side that cares the most about the deal or the potential deal, loses. If you are a buyer, be willing to walk. If you are a seller, be willing to lose the buyer. If you find yourself in a situation where you do care the most, for whatever reason, remain calm. And try not to communicate this to the other side.

~~~

As a broker and someone who grew up in the real estate business, I confess, I have a bit of a cavalier attitude: *There is always another house*. But if you can come to accept this gentle admonition, it will serve you well.

So don't fall in love with any particular house such that you might agree to something unreasonable or not in your best interest. And I do think this is mostly a question of attitude. Does the *perfect* house exist? And have you found it? We see this far too often. And when we do, more often than not, it is simply not true.

Rather, have a broader attitude: *Any number of houses will probably work for us*. This attitude gives you so much more leeway when it comes to negotiating. It gives you the freedom to walk away from any deal. That is real value.

Now sellers don't fall in love with buyers the way buyers fall in love with houses. Where we see this on the sell side is when a house is not moving and the seller says: Whatever we do, we don't want to lose *this* buyer. And that is understandable. But I would just caution sellers to not accommodate *a* buyer more than would be necessary to attract *other* buyers.

A simple example: You have a house that is not selling. And finally, you get a buyer asking for a $50,000 price reduction. But a $25,000 price reduction would more than meet the indicated value of all of the comps. Or some similar situation. You see what I mean.

Regardless of which side you are on, this factor can be hidden. And your broker may not have an incentive to bring it to your attention. A buyer gets into a bidding war and wants to overpay for his perfect house? That's fine with his broker. A seller is fed up with his house not selling and wants to take $25,000 less than he should? Again, fine with his broker. The buyer may not discover his error until he sells. The seller may never know.

Now, does it happen that a buyer finds, or thinks he has found, the *perfect* house? And he just has to have it. Of course. Let's be honest, this can happen to any of us. In this case, I think it is more important than ever to have a broker who will be honest with you. The broker should say: Look I understand the situation, but you must as well. If you want to proceed, we are both going to do this with our eyes open. Again, find an honest and objective broker.

So if you are a buyer who has found the perfect house or a seller with one and only one buyer, stop and reassess. And if you choose to proceed, do your best to not communicate this to the other side. That's really all you can do.

Finally, sometimes it is not about price. Maybe there is something unique about the property or the location that really just works for the buyer. But might be off-putting to most people. We see that. Or, and this is more frequent, a buyer is totally indifferent to some unattractive feature of the property. A common example here is: A small back yard. A particular buyer with no children may not care, but if it is a four-bedroom single-family house, most buyers will care a great deal.

In these cases, I like to remind the buyer, that one day, sooner or later, he will be the seller. *Everybody sells*. And if you don't sell, odds are your children will. So one day you will have to contend with that unattractive feature *as a seller*.

And I then ask: So, do you still want to buy it?

I tell buyers that overpaying for real estate is not a moral dilemma. It is perfectly okay to do so, so long as you know it in advance. It is not the broker's job to talk you out of buying it. Or, to stop you from overpaying. Or, taking less than you should as a seller. But it certainly is the broker's job to make sure you do so with your eyes open.

Chapter 40: Be Deliberate

Be deliberate. Do not be in a rush. Or at the very least, do not appear to be in a rush. Further, people have a natural tendency to prematurely accept the other side's terms. So be cautious of early or hasty acceptance.

~~~

We have discussed sellers' tendency to accept quick and early offers, often following their broker's advice. But in addition, regardless of which side you are on, the real estate process is a hassle. There is no getting around it. And people just want to get it done. So there is an incentive to rush the process.

Plus most Americans are not natural negotiators. Sure, we might haggle at a yard sale or when we occasionally go buy a car. But we don't haggle nearly as much as some other cultures. Consequently many people are intimidated by the negotiation process. And again, people just want to get it over with. This is not a revelation, we all know this is true.

So in the world of residential real estate, we see brokers rushing the process to get paid sooner and with the least effort, and we have buyers and sellers who just want to get it over with. So everyone is more than happy to achieve offer and acceptance…today.

And it is a shame because negotiations most often benefit from a slow and measured and deliberate pace. So when the other side says, *hey let's just split the difference*, you need not be in a rush to agree. Take the time to consider the question: Is splitting the difference a good deal for me? Or, maybe you'll split the difference on price, but you need a greater *Due Diligence Fee*. Or maybe, you need to think about what you need. I am not telling you to not take it. I am telling you to give yourself the time to consider it.

And when the broker says, well, we just got another offer. Or, we have more showings lined up this weekend. Or, we don't have any more showings scheduled. Whatever the case maybe, don't allow yourself to be ushered into a negotiation and then rushed through it.

What's that? They want to send over an offer tonight? Great, I'll look at it in the morning. How's that? They need an answer tonight? Why? They are considering another house? Well, if they absolutely need an answer tonight, they should probably buy the other one.

Think this is foolish? Well, if you can, I would encourage you to set the pace. Might you actually lose a buyer to another house tonight? Yeah, I guess it's possible. But likely not. The buyer is going to offer on the house that best meets his needs and desires, and if that house is yours, he will wait for your response. If not, likely the other house better meets his needs and desires anyway.

Are there circumstances where a buyer cannot wait? Sure. But they are much more rare than your broker would have you believe. Take a breath. Slow it down. Sleep on it. The fact that your broker wants to wrap this up in a couple of hours does not mean you have to do so.

Okay, but what if you are the buyer? And the broker says, there's another interested party who might make an offer. Tonight. Right? It happens. Should you break your pace and rush to counter? Well I admit, here the answer is trickier. And truthfully, there may not be a right answer. Just don't let rushed and impulsive trump deliberate and smart. I would add: Don't forget what you don't know. First, you don't know if there is, in fact, another interested party. Or another offer. Wait: Are you saying that a broker might lie about such a thing? Yes my friends, that happens. And even if there is another offer, you don't know how it compares to yours. We will come back to this in Chapter 48, Be Skeptical.

As an aside, I will tell you, if the seller says, *we have another offer*, and yet, this is the *one perfect house* for you, then it becomes immaterial whether you believe they have another offer or not. From experience, I have learned the hard way, that you must proceed as if there is another offer. And this is not a good position to find yourself in.

In any case, if you slow things down, you will make better decisions, and provide smarter and more thoughtful responses, for your own benefit. You just will.

My point is: If the choice is between possibly losing the other side (the house or the buyer) and taking more time, I come down on the taking more time side, every time. First, the choice is often contrived, and second, better and smarter are almost always better than rushed and impulsive.

But I guess we have to talk about the worst-case scenario: What if you do in fact lose the other side, and then there is not another forthcoming? The buyer bought another house or the seller took another offer. Your broker will certainly tell you that you should be concerned about this above all else. And the broker will add: You may not get another (house or buyer).

Well yes, sure, be aware that this is a possibility. But don't forget our previous chapter. You will do better, and you will negotiate yourself a better deal, if you don't care too much. Are there buyers and sellers who cannot afford to take this approach? Absolutely. But if you can afford it, I strongly encourage you to do so.

Chapter 41: On Seriousness

There is an inverse relationship between a buyer's represented urgency and their seriousness. There are exceptions, but this is true enough as a general rule.

Regarding viewings and inspections, there is a direct correlation between a seller's willingness to be accommodating and their seriousness. There are exceptions, but this is true enough as a general rule.

~~~

So you're selling your house and let's say showings have been slow, but you need it sold. You get a call from the showing service: Hey Mr. Seller, we have a buyer who would like to see your house. When? You ask. Well they are sitting outside in the car with their broker. But you are expecting guests for a dinner party any minute. Right? What to do?

So you say, I'm very sorry, but could you ask the buyer to schedule an appointment to see the place tomorrow. Anytime will be fine. And the response is: No they can't; they are flying out first thing in the morning. Right? What to do?

I urge you to enjoy your dinner party. Because in my experience the people who need to act right now, in this moment, turn out to be time wasters all the way around. It is fine if their impulsive desires do not involve you. But as in this example, so often they do. So interrupt your plans if you feel you must. But just don't be surprised if, at some point, and for some reason, it doesn't work out.

I refer to this as *represented urgency* because so often their actual urgency is something less than as represented.

Maybe even less than serious. Yes there are exceptions, but this is generally how it works out.

But okay, what if you are the buyer? And you are in town for a couple of days, looking for something to buy. And you've been out all afternoon with your broker, but nothing has really clicked for you. Right? So it's late and you are about to go back to your hotel because you are the one flying out first thing in the morning. But your broker says, hey let's swing by this one last house on the way. And you do and low-and-behold, it looks perfect. The broker calls to see if you can view it immediately. But the seller spouts some nonsense about a dinner party. Right? What to do?

Well there's not much you can do. But clearly, dinner party or not, the seller does not need to sell as much as you need to buy. That's a shame.

But wait: The seller is calling back. He says: Look, we like to sleep in Sunday morning, but if the buyer wants to come by on his way to the airport, we'll make that work. What time's his flight? Nine, fine, we'll be out of here by seven, and we'll leave the coffee on for you.

Well now, what does that tell you?

Now I know, these two examples are extremes. But you can tell quite a bit about the other side based on how accommodating they try to be. Serious buyers will be respectful of the seller, the seller's family and plans, and the seller's needs, and cognizant of the fact that the seller, you know, lives there. The serious buyer will do everything they can to work with the seller and around his schedule. Serious sellers will do likewise with potential buyers.

Both sides should be aware that buying and selling a home is a hassle, for themselves *and* for the other side. Obviously this is most true for occupied homes. But I have seen sellers decline potential showings for vacant property for no good reason. And I have seen buyers who are just unreasonable with their viewing expectations.

So as best you can, work with the other side. And if they seem unreasonable, well you know what? They probably are.

Chapter 42: Be Prepared

Be prepared. The side with the most knowledge does not always come out ahead, but it is a huge advantage. Read the contract, read the HOA documents, read the inspection reports, etc. Call the town, talk to the neighbors, get a survey, etc.

~~~

Yes it's a bit cliché, but be prepared. We've already talked about the contract. Read and understand that before you get started. But when you find something, read all the marketing material. It may be of limited usefulness, but it is readily and immediately available. Read the disclosures. There is usually a property disclosure and there may be others.

The homeowner's association (HOA) documents are important, especially for townhouses and condos. And any single family subdivision with lots of amenities or where the HOA owns and maintains the streets. You want to read the HOA documents to understand the procedures and the organizational structure. You want to read the recent HOA history to see what's going on and are there any possible assessments coming your way. A seller may be required to disclose confirmed assessments, but not a possibility that is currently under discussion. It would be a shame to close on a new home and then get hit with a $5,000 assessment at the next HOA meeting. Finally you want to have a look at their financial documents. You don't have to be an expert to notice that the reserves are underfunded. But if you need an expert, get one. Start with the HOA Property Manager; you never know how much she might be willing to share.

And you just never know what you are going to find. We once represented a buyer considering a house in a subdivision where a group of neighbors were suing the builder for failure to install a vapor barrier (house wrap) under the siding during construction. This may or may not be important to you, but do you want to get involved in a lawsuit of any kind? Seller disclosure: None.

Have the property inspected. These days, separate roof and HVAC inspections are quite common. Attend the property inspection and ask the inspector if he'd recommend separate inspections for these or anything else. Make sure to give yourself time to schedule these as needed.

A while back, ten years or so, lenders stopped requiring surveys for most residential properties. Certainly for the cookie-cutter neighborhoods. In any case, I am always amazed by how few people want a survey if the lender does not require it. But if the property you are considering has an encroachment, especially where it somehow encroaches on a neighbor, surely this becomes a negotiating factor.

And that busy road behind the property? Yeah, let's call the town and ask about that. What's that? They start the widening project next month? Did the seller disclose? Heck, did the seller even know?

You are walking out after viewing a home and along comes a lady walking her dog. Hey, do you live in the neighborhood; do you like it? Most people are happy to answer, good or bad. And if not, you have not lost anything. I am not saying that you need to go knock on doors. But if the opportunity to speak with a neighbor presents itself, be sure and take advantage of it.

On the sell side, I have a client who will research his buyers. Yes, they currently live here. Do me a favor and look up that house and see if it is for sale? Or, yeah, I found him on Facebook and LinkedIn. Looks like he got a job transfer to the area. Point is, he is not happy with the information provided with the offer and any lender documentation. He wants to know as much as he possibly can about who he is about to deal with. I mean he will send me articles from our local business journal: Hey, isn't this the guy who sent us the offer this morning? Necessary? Bit creepy? Or smart? You decide.

Now this is not meant to be a comprehensive list of what you should do when buying or selling a home. But clearly if you find that the HOA is considering a $5,000 assessment for street maintenance, that becomes a factor in the negotiation. You will either negotiate some portion of that off the price, or if you find that is not possible, at least you can proceed…if you choose to proceed, with full knowledge of what you are buying.

And truthfully, it is probably never enough. I have friends who bought a house in a neighborhood that backs up to an interstate-type divided highway. They were okay with that because there was a heavily wooded buffer between the houses and the highway. But some time after they purchased, low and behold, somebody started knocking the trees down. Soon enough they learned that the state transportation department had given the local power company an easement for new electric transmission lines. And they lost most of the buffer. Now could this have been determined ahead of time? Yes I think so. But I also think it is fair to ask: Would anyone think to check for this possibility?

Think about it. You lookup the subdivision plat. Nothing there, looks good. Yep, that's the state DOT that owns the land behind the subdivision, but we know there's a highway. Do you then pull the DOT surveys? Well if the buffer is important to you or your clients, you probably should. Another question of course is: Was the easement granted before or after they purchased their house? I don't know; thankfully, I was not involved. But I like to think that I would have been more careful. I hope so anyway.

Now my friends bought the house as new construction from the broker representing the builder. If the easement had been in place prior to purchase, then the broker failed to disclose a material fact, as they are required to do. So this would have been either negligent or willful *omission of a material fact*. Yes, it's a thing. But one take away from this chapter should be that we cannot depend on the other side to communicate any or all that they should (or that we might like them to). We must be prepared by doing our own homework.

So there are two lessons here. One, narrow, check out government-owned highway land for possible future utility easements. And two, more broadly, check out any adjacent or nearby land for anything vacant or odd or new. My advice: Go to the county GIS (Geographic Information System) and print out a half-mile radius of all the properties. I once did this and found a vacant parcel owned by the town, right next to the subdivision we were considering. Turned out the town had purchased for the possibility (not yet determined for sure) of placing a fire station on the parcel. Do you want to live next to a fire station?

Let me end this with one final story. My father was once part of an investment group that purchased a large tract of land outside of Myrtle Beach, South Carolina. After the purchase, they discovered two things: One, the land had been used as a practice bombing range in World War Two. And two, that there may be unexploded ordnance on the parcel. Here's the point: No one involved thought to ask the question: Could there be bombs on this land? No, the question just never occurred to anyone.

So it's probably just never enough. But the more you know, the better your negotiating position

Chapter 43: On Cultural Differences

Not surprisingly, people from different cultures have differing manners and attitudes about negotiation. Some purposefully more passive than what Americans expect; others quite a bit more aggressive. So it pays to do a bit of homework on this factor. But an understanding of the real estate process and contract is much more important than knowledge of cultural idiosyncrasies. In the end, they will use the same process and contract as anyone else.

~~~

We are constantly told that if we are dealing with people from foreign cultures, we need to be cognizant of cultural differences, in business generally, and in negotiations specifically. To use a fairly benign example, some Asian cultures do not use or appreciate a direct *no*. Rather *no* is couched in, *I'll have to think about it* or *I'll get back to you*, etc. Sometimes with an appropriate level of feigned embarrassment for good measure. It all has to do with saving face or providing the other party with the opportunity to save face.

And hey, I'm fine with that. If I know that I am going to be doing several deals with Japanese foreign nationals, I might even go out and buy a book on the subject: *Japanese-Style Negotiations,* or whatever. The Harvard Program on Negotiation offers: *International Negotiations: Cross-Cultural Communication Skills for International Business Executives.*[17] You get the idea.

---

[17] See the Program on Negotiation, Harvard Law School
https://www.pon.harvard.edu

And surely people from Latin America and Africa have their own cultural distinctions. And even within geographic regions, there will be differences. Think Japanese business culture as compared to, say, Philippine business culture. Or German compared to Greek.

Some of these differences can be quite interesting. And I know that studying these will help you with any cross-cultural negotiation. On the commercial side, I once served as tenant representative to a large Japanese chemical firm seeking an expanded office in our market. We looked at many possibilities, and a number of them would have worked. But in one of these, the landlord representative knew his Japanese business culture, and he nailed it, without overdoing it. He made subtle changes in his presentation and attitude, and I think that is what appealed to my client. And they leased space in his building.

So sure, if you know you have a client coming into town next week from Tokyo, why not give it a couple of hours? But if you wanted, you could spend all your time studying cultural differences. So how important is this type of thing on the residential side? Well we have bought and sold houses for people from all over the world: Europe, Latin America, Asia, Africa, and certainly the Indian subcontinent. And I would say knowledge of any specific cultural idiosyncrasy is less important than the simple respect that you would give any client. If you combine this with a natural level of sincere curiosity, you'll be fine.

Let me give you an example. There are many foreign nationals in our market, particularly from Asia. Early on, I dealt with clients searching for homes for whom the concepts of Feng shui were important. I knew absolutely nothing about it. Now I could have, and perhaps should have, gone out and researched the topic extensively. But I never did. Rather, when a client would say something would not work, I would be genuinely curious as to why. The clients felt I was listening and I did ultimately learn quite a bit about Feng shui. So that is my simple advice: Be respectful and be genuine.

But this is more important to understand: Regardless if the cultural difference is on your side, or the other side, or even on both sides, the real estate transaction is the same. Your Chinese clients may not accept a house with the front and back doors aligned or at the end of a street, but by golly, they are going to use the standard form contract. The Egyptian buyer on the other side may use family funds or some type of Sharia-compliant financing, but the real estate transaction will be very similar to a buyer from Omaha. The Indian buyers may have vastly more negotiating experience, and comfort with aggressive negotiation, than your typical American sellers, but they will tailor their efforts to fit the terms in the contract.

And in all of these cases you will find varying degrees of competence with the process and the contract. I know very little about Sharia finance. But that buyer better get it done before the expiration of the *Due Diligence Period*. Point is, if the broker does his job, these cultural differences take a huge backseat to transactional competence.

So whether the cultural difference is on your side or the other side, knowledge of these differences is less important than simple respect. And like any other deal, knowledge of the process and the contract remains paramount. Tip O'Neill liked to say that all politics is local. Well if there is anything more local than politics, it's real estate.

Chapter 44: Be Awake

Be awake. No one negotiates well when they are tired. And yet many residential real estate negotiations happen after work, in the evening, and sometimes late at night. Try to avoid this (on your side).

~~~

Clients cannot see houses if they are working. So brokers show a lot of property during evenings and weekends. That is to be expected. And some clients cannot break away during their work day for any non-work activity. I mean some clients will not even return your phone call until after 5:00 PM. So if they are buying a home for themselves, this process largely takes place at night and on weekends.

So a house pops up and your buyer clients want to see it… this evening after work. So you schedule a 5:30 PM showing and meet the clients at the house. This is the, what, twelfth house they've seen. And they like it. Sometimes they want to sleep on it and sometimes they want to make an offer. Tonight. So you write it up, have the client write some checks, and send it along to the listing broker. By this time it is after 8:00 PM.

Now if I happen to be that listing broker, it's easy. That's the end of it for the day. I am a morning person. I think most clearly early in the day. And I am going to deal with anything serious then. I may send the offer to the sellers, but I add: *Let's discuss this in the morning.*

But too often what we see is that a full scale real estate negotiation breaks out at 9:00 PM. Nine, because the sellers went out to dinner after work and just got in. So we are going to negotiate a $500,000 business deal starting at nine o'clock in the evening. I personally just find that to be insane.

And yet it happens all the time. And sure, sometimes, there are other offers involved. And the buyer fears, justifiably, that the seller may take another offer…tonight.

Questions: Why is the seller in such a rush? And why does the buyer panic? Come on, by now, you know the answer: Their brokers tell them to.

The listing broker tells the seller, look, if we don't get them locked down, the buyer may find something else. And the buyer's broker tells the buyer, we don't want them to take another offer. And if there is another offer, that broker is telling her buyers the same thing.

And look, you are not going to get the brokers to behave sensibly. Most will gladly work the deal until well after midnight and into the wee hours. Remember the brokers' priorities: Fast and easy and not necessarily best.

And so, even if one of the three parties is reasonable, they have to worry about the other two.

Anyway, this is the dynamic. You get the idea.

I would urge you, whichever side you are on, to…have a glass of wine. Pick it up in the morning. But like I said, the other brokers are going nuts; could you possibly miss out on this house or buyer? Yes. We discussed this possibility in our chapter *Be Deliberate*.

But in addition to setting a deliberate pace, I think we should also just ask the simple question: Are we awake? And I don't mean merely awake after dinner and a busy day at the office. I mean, are we fully awake? Bright-eyed and clearheaded? Are we awake enough to be negotiating a $500,000 deal with numerous moving pieces?

Let me put it differently: What if this was not your home that we were negotiating. Let's say, your boss gave you the task of negotiating the purchase of a $500,000 piece of equipment. Or, disposing of it. Either way. Would you, would anyone, deal with that at nine o'clock at night?

Yes, some might. They might take an equipment vendor out to dinner and negotiate the deal over cocktails. But they better be awake and clearheaded, because tomorrow morning they are going to have to explain that deal to their boss. The smarter thing to do is to schedule a meeting with the vendor for the next day. Skip drinks and dinner and get a good night's sleep.

But I think that's a problem with residential real estate: We are only accountable to ourselves. So fine: Hold yourself accountable and be smart. And don't allow your broker, or the other broker(s), to pull you into their frenzy.

Chapter 45: No Offer is Insulting

No offer is insulting. Period. Most of the time when sellers say that an offer is insulting, this idea comes from their non-business-savvy real estate broker. Be aware: Many financially able and savvy buyers will start low. So my advice is to always counter. But whether you counter or not, the correct response to ANY offer is: *Thank you very much for your offer*.

~~~

Could we start this chapter with a question: A little kid, a perfect stranger, approaches you and says: *You sir, are a stinky pirate*. Let's add the fact that there is no other person there to hear it. It is just you and the little kid. So the question is, are you insulted? Well sure, on the surface of it, maybe you are. But upon two seconds of reflection, I rather doubt it. First, it's a little kid who is a stranger. Second, does he even know what he is saying? And third, no one else heard it. If you are insulted by this scenario, I submit that there is more wrong with you than the unsupervised child. In other words, can you genuinely be insulted without credence or damage? That is, without credibility of the allegation or cost to you? Sure it is an insult, but you are not insulted.

Yet we see this sort of nonsense in the real estate business all the time. It goes something like this. A seller lists his $500,000 house for $525,000. And for this discussion, it does not matter whether that is a good starting price or not. But an offer comes in at $400,000. If this offer goes directly to the seller, there is what? Maybe a fifty/fifty chance that the seller would bother to counter. I mean time is valuable. But if the offer goes first to a broker, when submitting the offer to the seller, the broker sniffs: *This offer is insulting, I know you are insulted, it's not worth a response. I'll tell the buyer you're insulted.*

And often this will shut down any further discussion. I cannot tell you how often this happens in residential real estate. We'll come back to the broker in a minute. But for now, let me just ask: Should this type of thing insult a seller? Let's up the stakes, what if the offer is only $300,000?

Now the question here is not: Will some people be insulted? Because undoubtedly some will be. Rather, the question is: *Should* you be insulted? Well, could we think of this as we did the charge of being a stinky pirate: What is the credibility and what is the cost to you? And let's assume it is one hundred percent credible. An all-cash offer and the buyer includes a bank statement as proof of funds. The point is, this insulted business all revolves around the question of: What does this cost you, the seller?

I submit that it costs the seller nothing. What do you care if a buyer wants to spend his time and effort making a ridiculous $300,000 offer? Other than the time for a showing, and most showings produce absolutely nothing, the seller is not even out any time. If he chooses, the seller does not even have to take the time to read and consider the offer at all. So the offer may be insulting, but should the seller really be insulted? There is a difference.

Pride. Sometimes, that's the real issue. The buyer's $300,000 offer wounds the seller's pride. But if you are reading this book, and certainly if you have made it this far, I think you will know how silly this is. Pride has no place in a $500,000 business deal.

So take cost and pride out of it and what have you got? An offer. And what do we do with offers? We counter. Hey, I never said this was rocket science.

If you as the seller are at $525,000 and the buyer is at $300,000, sure you may not want to spend time on it. I get that. But if you have the time and inclination, why not give the buyer a counter? You don't even have to write it down. Call 'em up or shoot them a quick email. Say: Hey, got your offer; thank you so much for your interest. Yes, I see your proof of funds and I know you are serious. As a show of good faith on our side, we'll come down to $524,000.

Now I hear you: That's a waste of time. And if you feel that way, I am not here to talk you out of it. But I will tell you, I have been on the buy side with enough very shrewd and wily investor types to know that some people just have to start this way. It is who they are. And something else: I have seen some of them go on to actually overpay for property. Because where they start is not a valid indication of their actual interest. It's just not. In fact, the first offer is of no real significance. So why shut the process down before you find out what their actual interest may be?

And this brings me back to the inept brokers. I guess that is what this is: The brokers seem to believe that where the buyer starts is a valid indication of a buyer's interest. And if the buyer starts low, the broker is willing to totally dismiss the buyer regardless of actual interest, which remains unknown. And because the broker believes that starting price is a valid indication of interest, the broker makes no further attempt to discover the buyer's actual interest.

As for the broker telling a seller that an offer is insulting, well, that is merely a broker simply demonstrating that he or she has not thought this out. I also think that by telling a seller that an offer is insulting, the broker somehow thinks that she is proving her allegiance to the seller. But true allegiance would look like this: *Well Mr. Seller, I am not at all sure of what to make of it. But it's too early to tell; let's see where it goes.*

Of course, that takes a bit more effort…and a bit more smarts.

Chapter 46: Always Be Nice

Always be nice. I don't care if you are a world class reprobate, being nice is a proven negotiating tactic. Save your bad temper for the paperwork.

~~~

Buying or selling a home is different from buying or selling a rental property as an investment. For investment property, either the numbers work or they don't; it's rare to be exercised about it, much less emotional.

A home is different. A home is family and memories. Hopes and dreams. Aspiration and status and pride. Convenience and warmth and safety. Lifestyle. Even identity. A whole host of things beyond a simple black and white Profit and Loss Statement.

And it is important, even vital, to understand these attributes. What we are buying or selling goes beyond the building. It is the structure plus all of these intangibles.

So yes, emotions can run high. People can become angry or wistful or envious. And I guess that is natural. I am not here to tell you: Don't be emotional. Because perhaps that is unreasonable. But the fact is, emotions aside, we do want to get the best deal we can.

So even if you are angry or sad, do yourself a favor, and be nice. Because you will get a better deal for yourself if you are, or at least appear to be, nice and reasonable and calm. Certainly never voice your anger. If the other side says something, or does something, or proposes something, that makes you angry. Stop. Remain calm. Do not respond with an angry phone call or email. No response is better than an angry response. And besides, most often, whatever it is that makes you angry, does not, in fact, require a response at all.

But what if the other side is not nice? Yeah, we see this. While there are no hard and fast rules, I will let you in on something I have noticed over the years. There is a positive correlation between nice and smart. Or turn it around, a positive correlation between not very nice and not very clever; between rude and stupid. And often between rude and unprepared.

Even if someone is not very nice at heart, if he is at all clever, by golly, he has learned how to act nice. It is really only stupid people who never learn this lesson. So if someone is rude, that tells you a great deal about who you are dealing with.

So if someone is not nice, fine. It's all fine.

You will probably get a better deal. And you will not feel bad about taking advantage of their stupidity and unpreparedness.

Now do we need to talk about those few people who are rude and smart? Sure, I've met some. We all have. But they are so few and far between, I am not sure they merit a lot of thought. But if they have something you want, you may need to deal with them. Decide if it's worth it, and then just be prepared. Even with these types, I still find that I do best when I stay nice and keep calm. There is no point in escalating the rudeness. So if it is worth pursuing, keep your cool. Otherwise, just drop it and move on. We'll have more on this in our chapter on Difficult People.

But one note about this type of rudeness. Since these people are not stupid, where does their rudeness originate?

Well, it's an entitlement. These people are smarter or richer or better educated or speak with an Oxbridge accent. Or whatever. However they define it, they somehow believe that they are superior to you. And therefore, they are entitled to be rude to you. Otherwise, they simply would not be.

But notice the presumption here: These people may be smart, but they presume that they are smarter than you. Generally they are not. But even if they are, you can make up for it with experience and preparation. Since they don't expect it of you, often they are not properly prepared themselves. If they choose to underestimate you, hey, that's on them.

And really, this only applies to *smart*. Because if they are entitled to be rude because of their wealth or education, we are back to rude and stupid.

Enough rambling; you get the point.

The Andy Griffith Negotiation Strategy

Be Andy Taylor. You know, from Mayberry. Yes, let's think about how Sheriff Andy Taylor would buy or sell a house. He's folksy and open and kind. But not in a contrived way. No, he's genuine. But come on, we all know he is also clever and shrewd and…paying attention. He sets his own pace and never lets his emotions get the better of him. People often mistake easygoing for slow-witted or unimaginative. By the time the other side finally realizes who they're dealing with, it's all over. I am not saying to be someone you are not. Just take the Andy Taylor approach.

Ya'll come on over after church and get a good look at the place. After that we can chat a spell with some of Aunt Bee's cobbler.

In fact I like the Andy Taylor approach for all sorts of negotiations. Be open and kind and genuine and clever and shrewd and pay attention. Add folksy if you can be genuine about it. (If you cannot do folksy, be amiable. But everyone *can* be genuine.) Think about it: You can be all of these things, and at the same time, you can better understand the contract, and due diligence, you are better prepared, you are deliberate, and awake, and never insulted or emotional. You are accommodating, but with an ease that says, *weeell*, it doesn't really matter one way or the other.

See what I mean? It's a winning combination. Good negotiation is a combination of attitude and preparedness, and throw in a bit of intelligence and experience.

Chapter 47: The Golden Rule

The *Golden Rule* applies to negotiation and the entire real estate transaction. Do not lie about anything. If discovered, you will lose the goodwill of your counterparts and maybe the deal itself.

~~~

Treat others as you want to be treated.

Look it starts with being serious and accommodating and respectful and nice.

But in a real estate transaction, this is mostly about honesty. Do not lie about anything. Do not hide anything. Be open and honest about what you are selling. Or if you are the buyer, open and honest about your qualifications and how you are paying.

Fill out the disclosures as faithfully as you can. Don't move the sofa to hide the water stain. If there is an unnoticeable easement at the rear of the property, go ahead and disclose it. As a buyer, don't neglect to inform the seller that you must first sell your current house. If you are planning to use a lender, don't make a cash offer (yes, we see that).

Our firm feels most comfortable coming down on the side of over-disclosure. Question: But what if that hurts your position or even your clients? Well it can, and it might, and it will. And it has.

But our goal is this: Will the party on the other side be willing to deal with us again? Or even better, will they prefer to deal with us next time? And personally, I just sleep better if I know that I am an honorable person and an honorable dealmaker. It is as simple as that. And I don't find that corny one little bit. And certainly not naive. This *is* a book about integrity.

We have even gone so far to say to our clients: *Look, this disclosure is above and beyond what you are legally required to disclose. But we feel it is the right thing to do. We understand if you do not want to, but then you will need to hire someone else.* And yes, it has happened that clients have gone on to hire someone else. But we find that the type of people most likely to hire us fully support our position. And they are the type of people we prefer to deal with.

Plus this: Beyond the moral and ethical questions, it is also a practical position. In terms of risk management for our firm and for our clients, and in terms of staying out of court, and in terms of public relations and reputation, over-disclosure is the smart choice.

But now, notice what this is not. This is not: Make sure the other side gets as good a deal as you do. Rather it is: Give the other side the opportunity and information that you would want and need. What they do with it is beyond our control. Maybe that have a lot of experience. Maybe they do not. If not, maybe they are smart enough to get help. If they choose poorly and get less than competent help, well again, that is beyond our control. And we see it all the time.

I tell our agents that it is not our job to instruct the other side how to convey real property. If they don't know how to do it, there is help available. And it is certainly not our job to instruct a professional, a broker, how to convey real property.

The point is, we find that even with full and over-disclosure, we typically get the better deal.

Chapter 48: Be Skeptical

However, be skeptical of what the other side tells you. If the broker tells you that he just received another offer, well maybe he did and maybe he didn't.

~~~

So you finally found a house that meets your needs and desires. It's been sitting on the market for six weeks for whatever reason. But it ticks all of your boxes, so you make an offer.

But when you call the listing broker to confirm that he received it, he says: *Just so you know, there is another offer coming in.* Yes, after six weeks, he gets two offers on the same day; what are the odds? This once happened to me, as the buyer's broker, with a million dollar listing that had been sitting on the market over a year.

And here's the thing about that: There is absolutely no way to know whether or not the listing broker is telling you the truth. And, you will never know. But I suspect that there is a class of broker who always say this, as a matter of course, in order to get the buyer to up their offer. It is an effective ploy. And even better for the broker, It cannot be unmasked or policed. Because if necessary, the broker could write up his own, fake offer.

So as I said in our chapter *Be Deliberate*, if you want the house, you must proceed as if he is telling you the truth (because he may be). But here I just want to point out: Be skeptical.

If you can stomach it, the best way to deal with this situation is for the buyer to remember our chapter *Try Not to*

Care (Too Much). Call the listing broker back and withdraw your offer. There are two possibilities here: One, he is telling the truth. In which case as a buyer, you do not want to get in a bidding war and perhaps overpay. Because as you know, *there is always another house*. And two, he is not telling the truth. In which case, is this someone we want to be dealing with?

Then wait a bit. The house will either go under contract with the other offer…or, the listing broker will call you at some point and say the other offer fell through. Then you can decide whether or not the house is worth dealing with a maybe dodgy broker. At which point you might even decide to lower your offer price. Yes, this is no place for factitious shenanigans.

But of course this goes beyond the *other offer* hooey. What if the seller says: Yes, the house did have polybutylene pipes, but the previous owner replaced them. Notice how lets the seller off the hook regardless. I am not saying they are lying, I am just saying, be skeptical. Get an inspection. Same is true for any fact about the property. *Oh you noticed? Yes, that is a pig farm on the adjacent property, but we never smell it*.

But what about buyers? While buyers have less that we need to be skeptical about, they surely have some facts that we should not take at face value. This starts with the Pre-Qualification or Pre-Approval Letter. My goodness these things are most often not worth the paper they are written on. No, I am not saying they are *fake*. But the fact is they are not written by the decision maker(s). In other words, the lender-person (whatever his or her title) who writes the letter is never the underwriter.

Other buyer concerns may be proof-of-funds, contingent contracts, timelines and dates, and we have already discussed whether or not the buyer intends to honor the offer as written. Be skeptical and confirm anything that you can. Yes, call the brokers involved in the contingent sale, call the bank, etc. Do everything that you can.

Here let me just point out, if you are the seller, one way to insure buyer representations is to obtain an adequate *Due Diligence Fee*. Yes, the buyer's Pre-Approval Letter may well be worthless, but by golly if they don't proceed, you keep their money. In fact, I would go so far to say, if you get an adequate *Due Diligence Fee*, you worry less about even receiving a lender letter. This works for buyers as well: Yes, the seller may be less than forthright about the plumbing, and you are somewhat skeptical. So you will be conducting adequate and timely due diligence. And if you are not satisfied, you will exercise your right to terminate. So understanding and command of the due diligence provisions of the contract really help with this whole *be skeptical* attitude.

I am reminded of the seemingly ridiculous adage of Ronald Reagan: *Trust but verify*. Which of course just means *don't trust*. But I think what Reagan really meant was: Don't trust, but be as nice and respectful as you possibly can about it. Yeah, that works for real estate. All you can do is to make your verifications routine: Yes Mr. Seller, I did ask your neighbor about the pig farm…just routine.

Chapter 49: Excessive Talk & Clever Questions

People including most real estate brokers tend to talk too much. Just don't. No need to be taciturn, but do not be loquacious either. Rather, one might ask mild, unassuming questions. It is amazing what most people will answer and how much they will say.

~~~

People chat. People make small talk. And people *love* to chat about real estate. So when buyers and sellers meet, that is of course what they do. And you know another thing people like to talk about? Themselves. And this combination is…less than ideal.

Now some people who recognize this issue will handle it with quiet reserve. They are not rude, but they have their look and depart. They tend to ask very few questions; I think out of fear that questions may lead to a conversation which they are trying to avoid. And in the process of a modern real estate transaction, buyers and sellers most often don't even meet until the closing.

Personally, I think this is an opportunity lost. It is possible to have a conversation and say very little about yourself. And it's easy: Just put these two things (talk about real estate and talk about themselves) together and ask questions. Like: *How long have you lived here? Why are you selling?* Unassuming and disarming questions. *How should we proceed? What are your thoughts?* Or even: *I'm not sure, what are your thoughts?* Don't be pushy about it, take a rather relaxed approach. And you will have to reciprocate. But ask one question at a time and give them time to answer. Never answer the question for them.

Most people understand that if they are buying or selling real estate, it is probably best to not talk too much. But human nature being what it is, often times people just can't help themselves. So ask questions, answer politely as necessary, and then ask more questions. The point is, just give people the opportunity to talk. They love it.

But there is one thing to point out about these questions. Let's use a common example: *Why are you selling?* If it is for a good reason, they might tell you. *Yeah, I got a big promotion and a job transfer to Albuquerque.* But they're not going to tell you a bad reason: *I lost my job and we just can no longer afford the place.* So if we can get them, we do care what the answers are. But we are also interested, perhaps more interested, in the conversation around the answers. While they're preoccupied in not answering your particular question, they may very well tell you something else. So listen closely. Yes again, it's not rocket science.

If you are dealing with the other side's broker, the same applies. They'll chat if given the opportunity. Here's a little trick: Ask the broker for her advice. But not about this property. For example: What do you think about ABC neighborhood? Or, have you ever sold a house in that neighborhood? What do you think about all the new houses built on slabs? What do you think of Toll Brothers as a builder? Do you know a good real estate attorney?

Two things: First, just get her to chat with you (hopefully, off-script). And two, all brokers want clients. And no matter what else you may be, to a broker, you are a potential client. Either in a dual agency situation for this property or as a client for some other property.

Now all brokers *should* take the position that when working on behalf of client X, if they are dealing with you as a potential buyer or seller, they should not attempt to make you client Y. This way they will be solely focused on serving X's interests. I would label this a *best practice*.

But this is just not the way brokers think. So use the broker's innate desire to acquire you as a client in order learn more about her existing client or the property. Set the pace; don't be in a hurry. I am not saying to waste your time, or even the broker's time; this is not that sort of game. Rather, this conversation is fairly subtle and cannot be rushed. But if a broker sees an opportunity to acquire you as a client, she may be careless, sometimes even reckless.

Now, is this a bit devious? Well don't lie to her and don't mislead her. If you are worried about this, just stick with questions. But allow her to do what comes naturally: Job Number One, Client Acquisition. And notice this: If the broker is doing her real job, serving and protecting the interests of her client, this little trick will not work. You will notice this right away because her attitude will be: I am not here to give you free advice; go hire your own broker. Right? Of course.

In fact, the only time these brokers do not view you as a potential client is when you are the broker on the other side. In which case, you cannot use her desire to acquire you as a client to your advantage.

But most brokers care a great deal about what other brokers think of them. They should not, but they do. They want validation and respect from other brokers. So take the chummy colleague approach. The two of you share a knowledge, a certain insight, that your respective clients just cannot appreciate. Yes, it's a burden you share. So treat her like a valued partner. Sometimes even, treat her with the deference due a valued senior partner. She'll love it.

Look, if she's competent, this probably won't do you any good, but it will not hurt. If she is not competent, she will appreciate the fact that you think she is, and treat her like she is. She certainly believes herself to be competent (because everyone does). I have been utterly amazed at what some brokers will reveal to me (as the opposing broker) with this approach and a little chitchat, respect, nurturing, and commiseration. It does not always happen. But it happens enough that it is worth a try.

And even when chatting with other brokers, brokers are like anyone else. If you ask for their advice, they will be flattered. You must be genuine; so pick something that you really need advice on. And if you are working in the real estate business, there is always something that you need advice on. Hey, do you know a good attorney in Anytown? Have you ever dealt with X issue? Ask her about her firm. Heck, ask her about her new car. Remember, she is a valued partner, maybe even a valued senior partner. Just make it about some other issue than the property under consideration. Because I promise, she will come back to it.

Keep in the back of your mind that brokers want to make a deal, any deal, more than they want to make the best deal. So be friendly and respectful, even deferential if it works, while at the same time you are better prepared, have complete command of the contract tool, take full advantage of the due diligence provisions, set the pace, all of it.

Chapter 50: Discussion is Not Always Helpful

During a transaction, at the first sign of trouble, move communications to writing, preferably email. Trouble can take any form. Examples: Hostile, aggressive, prickly, or belligerent counterparts. Writing is also a good way to deal with the scripts discussed earlier. Discussion is not always helpful; if necessary, shut it down.

~~~

We talked about scripts in the Broker Section. But you may be surprised to learn that the script-readers will even attempt to use their scripted nonsense on other brokers. I have no idea how successful they are with this charade on other brokers, but personally I have no patience for it.

So how do I deal with it? I stop taking their phone calls.

Scripts work best in a conversation (well a scripted exchange). So in person or on the phone. And while discussions are the easiest way to conduct real estate business and move transactions forward, the whole thing, all of it, can be dealt with via email. These days I would add, cautious use of texting. I say cautious because texting is more conversational.

The first thing to note about email and texting is it becomes perfectly easy to set the pace. You cannot easily halt or delay a phone conversation, but by golly, emails and texts only transmit if and when you hit send. But of course the greatest benefit of this approach is you are denying the script-reader the control that they so desperately seek.

Having a conversation with these people is not helpful or productive. So just don't. Oh, you will most often continue to get voice mails, and you can hear the frustration in their voice. Frustration that they are not in control. But just respond with another email or text. Or don't.

Now some people seem to believe that the negotiation process is a battle. A game or competition of aggression. And the most combative side will win. Aggressive as in rude and belligerent, sometimes even with a bit of shouting. I am not sure, and it certainly does not matter, if these people really are inherently rude or if it is just a game they are playing, or a role they are assuming. Either way, it's fine. Remember, they may have something you want. So just walking away is not always an option.

Remain calm, and again, stop taking their phone calls. Move all responses to email and text. While the rudeness may well continue in written form, you will certainly be setting the pace and more likely be in control. It will drive them crazy. But you stay calm and in control and continue moving the process forward.

We once dealt with a broker who was quite rude and belligerent. So after moving all discussion to written form, he threatened us: You will either take my phone calls or I will report you to the Real Estate Commission. I guess he felt that it was his right to be rude. But one other nice thing about moving conversations to written form is that they are now recorded and documented. I am not saying that the rudeness will stop. But I am saying that there is now a record of it, should you ever need it.

Further, as we discussed in our chapter Always Be Nice, there does seem to be a correlation between nice and smart.

Many of the jerks make mistakes. So watch for them, protect your interests, and now you'll have a record if needed.

Of course this strategy works for any number of bad actors with bad attitudes. Some people are hostile. Yes, even while they supposedly want to make a deal. We get prickly and whiny and passive-aggressive and overly anxious. Know-it-alls, yup can work with them too. It is just a good all-around strategy for dealing with troublemakers and mischief of any kind.

Chapter 51: Difficult People

People who are difficult to deal with on the front end will be difficult all the way through the transaction. Decide early how much you are willing to tolerate.

~~~

This often starts with failure to be accommodating. Then, they're not nice or easily insulted or they want everything yesterday. Whatever the case may be. Some people are just difficult to work with. And generally, the best way to deal with people like this is to, not deal with them.

Now we all deal with the rigamarole and rudeness and arcane bureaucracy at the DMV. Because they have something we want, in fact, something we need. And if we are clever, we even learn ways of dealing with the foolishness in order to most quickly and efficiently achieve our goals, with as little frustration to ourselves as possible. But question: Would we deal with their nonsense if we did not have to? No. They get away with their bad behavior because they know full well that we are a captive audience. And by golly, we need them, more than they need us. In fact, they don't need us at all. And that is basically their attitude.

Contrast this with the people we deal with in the real estate business. What would they have to have in order for us to give them the same deference that we give the lady at the DMV?

Well it certainly happens. We once dealt with a seller who had a single-floor unit for sale in a mostly two story townhouse complex. It was the first one to come on the market in over five years. And my clients wanted and needed it for an elderly parent. But the seller was quite rude and made ridiculous demands from the get go. And because we wanted it so badly, we acceded to the seller's every ridiculous demand and tolerated every discourtesy.

But a couple of points. First, if they start rude, most often the rudeness will continue right through the closing. And two, you just have to decide how much you are willing to tolerate. And the earlier you make this decision, the better.

But I hear you. You say, but if you suck it up, you get what you want. Be a grownup. Right? Of course. And often that is the smart strategy. But let's go back to our townhouse. They were quite rude *and* we ended up overpaying. Now, we did not overpay because they were rude. No, but we overpaid for the same reason that we tolerated the rudeness: They had something that we desperately wanted. Then a couple of years later, my client's elderly parent died, and we took a rather large loss on the unit.

Here's my point: In the real estate business, it should be extremely rare for you to be willing to deal with difficult people. Sure, if you are in this business for any length of time, you will have to. But each and every time that you face this issue, I would just suggest that you ask the questions: How much do I want or need this? And how much bad behavior am I willing to tolerate in order to get it? Are there any viable alternatives?

We have talked about the correlation between nice and smart, and rudeness and stupidity. But I also think that someone who is rude is more likely to waste your time. Believe me, if someone is entitled to be rude to you, they are certainly entitled to waste your time. So unless you are a masochist, you gain nothing by tolerating their rudeness.

After a few experiences like this, one tends to become rather intolerant of bad behavior. And I think that is a beneficial and even healthy attitude to develop in the real estate business.

I don't really deal with many residential rentals. But after the downturn in 2008, many of us did have to do a bit of leasing. I will never forget a series of phone calls I got from a potential renter. She started very rude, and I shut the phone call down right away. But then she proceeds to call me back multiple times, ending, of course, with a threat to call the Real Estate Commission. I encouraged her to do so, and even gave her the phone number. But the point is: Even if she was not wasting my time, can you imagine dealing with such a person over the course of a twelve-month tenancy?

I had a guy call me about a house for sale. Same deal, quite rude and condescending. But it had been a long listing and we definitely needed a buyer. So even though he was quite rude, I agreed to show him the place the next day. But an hour later, I called him back and canceled. I told him: I think you are wasting my time, and even if you are not, I just don't want to deal with you. I never regretted that decision.

One final perhaps less egregious example. But I think it demonstrates where you need to get, attitude-wise. Another potential tenant calls me about a rental unit. Wants to see the place after work, at 5:30. So I am there at twenty after, because, you know, he might be early, and contrary to how this chapter sounds, I am in fact very customer service oriented. Anyway, he never shows, no phone call, nothing. I leave at six.

Two days later he calls me: Hey, couldn't make it the other day; can I see it this evening after work, at 5:30? Right? My response: Absolutely, but you need to first come to my office before five o'clock, and bring me $100, in cash. He said, well I'm not sure that I am going to rent the place and I don't want to pay the application fee until I am sure. I said, well our application fee is sixty dollars. No, this hundred is to compensate me for my time, fifty dollars for the other day and another fifty dollars for today. Needless to say, he found that ridiculous and I never heard from him again.

But again, even if he was not wasting my time, can you imagine dealing with that guy as a tenant? And here's another important point: The next week, I rented the place to nicest young couple. And they were perfect tenants. Imagine that.

Chapter 52: The *No Response* Response

Remember that one legitimate form of response is: No response. Tactically, this can be very effective.

~~~

Regardless of what type of negotiation is going on and of the attitude and experience of your counterparts, sometimes you reach an impasse. This can be about *Purchase Price* or any other term(s) important to both parties.

If you can manage, the best position in any negotiation is when the other side wants to make a deal more than you do. Remember Try Not to Care (Too Much). Now you want to make a deal, of course you do, but your attitude is: Well, if this does not work out, there will be other alternatives. Right? But at the same time, you would prefer not to start again from scratch. What should you do?

Concede? Again, this is not a moral dilemma. Sometimes this is simply the practical or efficient thing to do. So I am not here to tell you this is the wrong thing to do. But I hope this book has given you some alternatives.

One thing you could do is: Simply don't respond to the other side's last counter. This can be particularly effective if negotiations, to this point, have been proceeding at a rather brisk pace. Don't explain, just stop.

First, a change of pace is always striking. It will get their attention. And second, put yourself in their shoes. Would you not worry that you had overdone it? Pushed too far, tried to get too much. Turned off the other side. And you might also worry: Geez, I wonder if they are reconsidering alternatives? The delay alone might make you nervous.

Right? So sometimes it can be effective to let the other side worry a bit. And yes, some people will worry more than others. And of course some will not worry at all, and for them this tactic will not be effective. But it is fair to say that most people will worry to some extent.

So the question then becomes: So how long do we let them stew? And there is no right answer. You just have to feel your way. Here, there is no substitute for experience. Sometimes it's a few hours, sometimes overnight will get the job done.

Let me add here that you can halt communication, or you can halt negotiation, or both. But any longer than 24 hours, it is probably, but not always, best to continue communication with: *Well, we're still thinking about your last counter*. Then of course you might get: *Well, when can we expect your answer?* Again, feel your way, because the best response might be: *It's hard to say*.

If you really don't care too much and want the absolute best deal you can get, stop both indefinitely, and wait for them to change or improve their last counter. Don't say *no*; rather don't say anything.

Now, of course, this is risky business. So if you need the deal to work, I don't recommend this sort of thing. But if you can afford to play hardball, this can be an effective way to do it.

One final note on this tactic. Remember so many brokers are not business savvy or have limited business savvy and experience. So the broker's reaction is difficult to predict. But in my experience, it is rarely: *Oh, these guys are playing hardball; this is just part of the negotiating process.* That's certainly what I would think. But no, with brokers, the reaction is typically: *I have never experienced such rudeness*. It never seems to occur to him that this is part of the process. And remember, he wants and expects quick and easy. Point is, don't be surprised if a broker calls you rude. But then you cannot say: *Well, you know, we are in a negotiation*. So if you must talk with him, be conciliatory and assure him that you are still interested. Don't allow his ineptitude to get in your way.

My suggestion: Don't take a rhinestone cowboy to a gun fight. Want to play hardball, find a gunslinger.

Chapter 53: Watch Your Net, Not the Details

Financially, real estate negotiating is a zero-sum game. Do not focus on where every dollar is gained or lost. Focus on your net.

~~~

In a real estate deal, hopefully both the buyer and the seller get what they want. So one can make a very strong case that this is not a zero-sum situation. Both parties gain. And this chapter is not intended to challenge that.

Rather here, let us look at the negotiation that takes place from a financial perspective. Remember, it takes place on a platform, the standard form offer and contract, with or without any additional addenda. And however long and detailed the resulting document may be, it is a finite agreement with a finite set of terms, and certainly a finite set of financial terms.

Is it possible that a term, or a negotiated change in a term, can benefit both parties? Absolutely. But most often, terms or changes benefit one party or the other.

And it is easy to get bogged down in each and every term. How much do we gain here? How much do we lose there?

Now one negotiating approach would be to address each and every term, driving all of them individually in your favor. Of course you can do this, but you run the risk of your counterpart feeling abused, or worn down, or even beaten up. And they may become defensive. So this strategy may actually work against you. And some people get rattled by even the most seemingly innocuous details.

The point here is to worry less about each and every term, and more about the net result. But we take it a step further.

Our practice is to write the cleanest possible offers with the fewest possible terms. Obviously this is done on a case by case basis, but our goal is always the same.

Maybe an example is in order. Sure as a buyer, you are going to propose a *Purchase Price*, but need you ask for a $1,000 home warranty? Or, for the seller to include his obviously brand new appliances or patio furniture? Do you really need the seller to pay $5,000 of your closing expenses?

This simplifies the offer. And because of that, it allows you to say to the other side: *You'll notice how clean and simple our offer is. We really want to make this deal work.*

So give them an offer with as few detailed terms as possible, because the details are subject to further negotiation. If it is the other side adding the details, hold firm on the major terms and ask them to drop the smaller ones. Say: *Well, you could get your additional $1,000 over here.... Let's make this as clean and as simple as possible. Because we really want to make this deal work and we know you do too.*

Now why is this important? I think most people, including many brokers, just find the real estate negotiation process intimidating. And therefore, they respond positively to *simple*. Or well, *simpler*. Plus some people will view the smaller terms as an attempt to get a better deal. And while they may or may not be watching their own net, they will be concerned that all this little stuff is adding up. So remove their concern.

In any case, you don't really care one way or the other. Because from start to finish you are only looking at your net figure. If people respond well to simple, and most do, fine give them simple. If you can, remove their concerns. Not for their benefit, but for ours.

Are there people who want, even insist on, all the little detailed terms? You bet. But again, worry less about each detail and focus on your net. Plus notice this: If they insist on some detail, ask yourself why. Maybe they really need (not *want*, but *need*) you to pay $5,000 of their closing costs. In which case, it is probably worth more, to the buyer, than $5,000, in other terms. So it is possible to accede to their request and your net still goes up.

The reverse is also true. If new appliances would cost the buyer $2,000, but he would accept the seller's set, surely this is worth a thousand dollars to the buyer, in some form or another. Again, his net goes up. And I am always surprised how often the sellers will let go of appliances or other assets for little or nothing.

One final point, sometimes what the other side requests may be quite valuable to them, but costs you very little. An example: It is not worth moving your patio furniture across the country and you were planning on giving the furniture to your brother-in-law. Right? But if the buyer is asking for them, maybe you agree if the buyer drops his request for that expensive home warranty. Simplifies the deal and you come out ahead. You may be surprised at how frequently these opportunities present themselves. Watch for them.

So in a real estate negotiation, this is just good psychological and financial strategy and practice. Notice also that it will appeal to the quick and easy brokers. Watch your net and give them what they want.

Chapter 54: Better Than Expected Offers

From time to time you will receive offers or counter-offers that are better than they should be, especially from inexperienced or unprepared counterparts. Focus negotiation on enforceability and execute quickly.

~~~

I listed a large house on a small lot. It essentially had no back yard. That's a tough sale. And it took the better part of a year to sell it (March to December). But in November, the first and only offer finally arrived.

The subject of the back yard never came up. I truly believe that for these particular buyers, it was not an issue. And their broker, God bless him, did not warn the buyer, that one day they will be the seller (we talked about this in Chapter 39).

The point is, we were quite happy to get an offer. And when it came in, it was close to our *Purchase Price*. And here is the real kicker, it included a $2,000 *Due Diligence Fee*. You remember, this is the nonrefundable amount paid directly to the seller. Now for the price point of this house, a $2,000 *Due Diligence Fee* was a dream come true.

So we negotiated, a bit, on the *Purchase Price*, and never discussed the *Due Diligence Fee*. Easy deal.

Yes of course, too easy. Because during the *Due Diligence Period*, the buyer had the place inspected. Several inspections actually. And based on his inspections, he asked the seller for a large discount on the *Purchase Price*.

Now this was a house in very good shape. And when the request came in, for a $15,000 discount, I immediately wondered if the buyers ever had any intention of honoring the deal as negotiated. I just don't think so; they knew that they would get another bite at the apple. And I guess most people who think this way seem to believe that by the time this happens, the seller will agree just to get it done, especially so late in the year. This is a hardball tactic, and it often works because too many incompetent listing brokers allow their sellers to get into a weak negotiating position. We talked about this extensively in our chapter on Negotiating Due Diligence.

And here, given the circumstances, the seller might very well have agreed. But these buyers were too clever by half. They had offered and the sellers had accepted the $2,000 *Due Diligence Fee*. With no discussion whatsoever. So when we discussed it, I asked the sellers to consider how much the buyer had spent on this property that they would not and could not recover. And we estimated (because we cannot know) this amount to be around $3,000.

Now let's stop here and point out that $3,000 is an order of magnitude less that the buyer's requested discount. So in a rational world, the buyer would be willing to walk away from $3,000 rather than spend fifteen thousand on *repairs*.

But while that may be true, it is still $3,000 out of the buyer's pocket. And if the buyer does walk, he will have to come up with additional funds for the next house (although by then he will have learned his lesson on how much of a *Due Diligence Fee* to offer). Isn't it a shame that his broker failed to adequately advise on this topic?

Now I have had buyers walk away from as much as a $5,000 *Due Diligence Fee*. So it can happen. But in our experience it is very rare for a buyer to walk away from a four-figure *Due Diligence Fee*. It is worth pointing out that for the price point of this house, we would have accepted a one thousand dollar *Due Diligence Fee*. We only got two thousand because that was what the seller offered, and it was never discussed.

But if all of this is only a game to allow for a re-negotiation of the *Purchase Price*, the fifteen thousand figure is not real anyway. But you know what is quite real? The $3,000 already spent and nonrecoverable.

It is interesting to point out that the three thousand dollars is a *sunk cost*,[18] and therefore, should not be a relevant factor in the decision to move forward. But there are a number of other factors which keep it relevant. First, it still has utility because the *Due Diligence Fee* is applied to the *Purchase Price* at closing. Second, the buyer may or may not have more cash, or enough cash, for an alternative property. And three, we are comparing a very real cost with one that may or may not be real. Well, I think it is interesting anyway.

So what did our seller do? Well she is one of my shrewdest and most savvy clients. She offered a $1,000 discount on the *Purchase Price* and told the buyers to take it or leave it. And she held fast.

There was much consternation on the buy side. Think about it, the buyer never had any intention of paying the agreed upon *Purchase Price*. And now they are faced with

---

[18] I found a nice, straightforward definition of sunk cost in the Encyclopædia Britannica: In economics and finance, a cost that has already been incurred and that cannot be recovered. In economic decision making, sunk costs are treated as bygone and are not taken into consideration when deciding whether to continue an investment project.

Peter Bondarenko, Encyclopædia Britannica, 7 October 2019.
https://www.britannica.com/topic/sunk-cost

the very real possibility that they are going to lose their three thousand dollars.

They threatened us with termination, which was their right. We took it in stride. And then the phone calls became aggressive and angry, so we stopped taking them. But the threatened termination never came.

And that is the end of the story. The transaction did close. With the one thousand dollar discount; no repairs were made. My client was tickled pink.

Chapter 55: On Win-Win

Finally, something should be said about the whole *win-win* negotiating construct. If the other side says, *we're looking for a win-win deal*, the only possible response is, *yes absolutely*. And to the extent that understanding what the other side wants helps us get what we want, that is true. But the fact is that most deals do not turn out as *win-win*. Anyone who tells you otherwise is naive, inexperienced, or lying. Deal with this as you think best.

~~~

I have always been leery and skeptical of win-win negotiating, and suspicious of those who espouse it, particularly for residential real estate transactions. I remember reading the win-win bible, *Getting to Yes* [19] back in the Nineties. Brought to us by the good academics at the Harvard Negotiation Project. I found it unsatisfying and terribly naive despite, as Jim Camp describes win-win, *its omnipresence in our culture*. Certainly *Getting to Yes* is omnipresent in negotiating circles.

We will come back to my concerns in a minute. For now let's turn to Camp, the primary opponent and skeptic of win-win, and his own work on negotiation fundamentals and strategy, *Start with No*.[20] Camp offers an alternative to the win-win ideal. I am not sure if Camp intended his title to be a reproach to the Harvard title, *Getting to Yes*, but I always read it that way. Harvard: *Getting to Yes*; Camp: Yeah well, *Start with No*. I love it.

---

[19] Roger Fisher, William Ury, and Bruce Patton, *Getting to Yes: Negotiating Agreement Without Giving In*, Second Edition. Houghton Mifflin, 1991.

[20] Jim Camp, *Start with No: The Negotiating Tools That the Pros Don't Want You to Know*. Crown Business, 2002.

Before you even crack the book open, right there on the jacket we find a nice summary:

> For years now, win-win has been the paradigm for business negotiation – the *fair* way for all concerned. But don't believe it. Today, win-win is just the seductive mantra used by the toughest negotiators to get the other side to compromise unnecessarily, early, and often. Have you ever heard someone on the other side of the table say, "Let's team up on this, *partner*"? It all sounds so good, but these negotiators take their naive *partners* to the cleaners, deal after deal...Win-win plays to your emotions. It takes advantage of your instinct and desire to make the deal.[21]

You can immediately see how the win-win strategy would appeal to real estate brokers. It's just so friendly and fair and not intimidating; and more importantly for brokers, facilitates a quick and easy deal. No doubt Fisher and Ury and other win-win proponents would argue, *but that is not the purpose of our work*. Perhaps not, but any experienced negotiator will tell you, that is how it is used.

Here's Camp:

> The unspoken – or sometimes spoken – assumption behind win-win is that people enter negotiations trying to build friendly relationships and want to leave with that relationship intact. The classic win-win dilemma is this one: *How much money do I have to leave on the table in order to maintain this relationship?* Big-time corporate

---

[21] Ibid, dust jacket. Is there a formal procedure for citing a book's dust jacket? I am not sure. I am also not sure who wrote the jacket copy. The author? It is doubtful. Probably some Random House employee (Crown is an imprint of Random House).

negotiators, along with many others, play this game to the hilt. They play up the importance of partnerships, loyalty, the long term – emotion-based stuff. *How could you endanger such benefits by holding the line?* But their only real concern is the price they're paying.[22]

In other words, savvy, and yes some predatory, negotiators take advantage of the naïveté of the win-win crowd. And they play them for saps.

Returning to my own thoughts on win-win negotiating, I just find that it is not very practical. Typically one side cares more about a deal than the other. One side has more experience or greater preparation than the other. One side has a *Client Acquisition* broker and the other has a *Conveying Real Property* broker. One side is accommodating and easy to deal with; the other not so much. One side wants a quick and easy deal done by midnight; the other side is more deliberate. One side talks too much and the other side asks clever questions. One side has a business savvy broker with good technical skills, the other does not. You get the point.

So in my experience, the only way to arrive at a win-win deal is when both parties are equally balanced between wants and desires, experience, preparation, command of platform, understanding of due diligence, and general negotiating competency, etc.

And how often does that happen?

Stop. Really, think about this: How often does that happen?

---

[22] Ibid, page 61.

If you are in the superior position with the proper attitude, or you are the more accomplished or prepared negotiator, are you going to give up your position or experience to *merely accept* a win-win deal? Remember as a fiduciary, it is your job to get the best deal for your client while also protecting their interests, and maintaining your principles and integrity. That is your job. That is competent negotiating.

Now let us not forget Jim Camp's point, that many very savvy negotiators who advocate for a win-win deal just want to take advantage of a less-savvy counterpart.

That means that there are three types of negotiators who bring up win-win. First, those naive enough to really believe in win-win. Second, the predatory types who want to take advantage of a not-so-savvy counterpart. And three, the script-readers who have given very little, if any, thought to the concept, but have been taught that *win-win* works well (sounds good) in a script.

Let us forget the first and assume that every time we hear the words *win-win*, we are dealing with the predators or script-readers. So when we hear *win-win*, it becomes a red flag. Give them a *yes absolutely*. Then ignore it. And do everything we have discussed in this section.

I have found that the predatory types are typically not as savvy as they think they are – Certainly not if they are merely looking for an easy route to take advantage of their counterparts. Certainly not once we recognize the win-win shtick. Allow them to underestimate you; they do so at their peril. As I said at the end of our chapter Always Be Nice, by the time they realize who they are dealing with, it's all over.

Yes, sometimes we see the predators in residential real estate negotiations. But a more common dynamic is this: On the one side, pushy script-readers with their rush to close, quick and easy, all the while talking a good win-win game. And on the other side, calm, deliberate, prepared, competent negotiators, never insulted or emotional, who don't care too much, and call back the next day.

In which case, the odds of a win-win deal are practically zero.

Conclusion: Gresham's Law for Real Estate

The incompetent, low integrity brokers drive out the competent, high integrity brokers. Those brokers who focus on client acquisition drive out the brokers who focus on conveying real property.

~~~

In economics, Gresham's Law is a monetary principle that states: *Bad money drives out good*. So for example, if you have quarters made with silver and quarters made with nickel, but all quarters are worth twenty-five cents, the silver quarters will begin to disappear (because people hoard them for their intrinsic value and use the nickel coins for daily transactions).

Now Thomas Gresham was a sixteenth century English merchant and financier, and this principle was actually named for him three hundred years later, by nineteenth century Scottish economist, Henry Dunning Macleod, in 1860. But of course, as all coinage today is intrinsically worthless, the monetary value of Gresham's Law is purely academic.

But let's move forward about sixty years to a passage by former Canadian Prime Minister Mackenzie King. Please indulge me, his language is somewhat dated:

> Something analogous to Gresham's Law will be found to obtain in the case of competing standards in Industry. Assuming there is *indifference* in the matter of choice between competing commodities or services, but that in the case of such commodities or services the labor standards involved vary, the inferior standard, if brought in this manner into competition with a higher standard, will drive it out, or drag the higher down to its level. This

is effected by the opportunity of under-selling which comes, where in such cases human well-being is sacrificed to material ends. The superior standard, *not being recognized or demanded*, is unable to hold its own, and in time disappears. This Law is just as real and relentless in its operation in Industry as Gresham's Law of the precious metals is with respect to money and the mechanism of exchange. Indeed, a more accurate exposition would describe both as manifestations of one and the same law, which I propose to call the Law of Competing Standards.[23] [Emphasis added]

So in broader terms, Gresham's Law can be applied to any circumstance where true value is different from that which people are required to accept, or are simply willing to accept, or perhaps even blindly accept. King points to *indifference*, but it can be due to any number of factors including lack of information, knowledge, experience, or even corruption, deceit, or pretense. Plus a lack of enforced standards (and ethics), consequence, or penalty.

That is to say, if we make no distinction for the worthy and no penalty for the unworthy, the unworthy proliferates, and over time becomes the new standard.

Let's move forward, again about another sixty years, to Charlie Munger. For those of you who do not know, Charles Munger is Vice Chairman of Berkshire Hathaway. Munger offers a simple modern update and expansion of Gresham's Law. He called it a new form of Gresham's Law, but personally, I think of it as Gresham's Law for Our Age: *Bad*

---

[23] Mackenzie King, *Industry and Humanity: A Study in the Principles Underlying Industrial Reconstruction.* Houghton Mifflin, 1918.

morals drive out the good. Unethical behavior is contagious.[24]

Here Farnam Street offers an excellent descriptive example:

> This can be common in some business fields. Take two drug salespeople – one willing to bribe doctors to make sales, and one not willing to do so. If the industry functions such that fraudulent business practices *are not punished*, and the bribery goes uncovered by the buyer's organization, then bribery obviously gains a sustainable competitive advantage over non-bribery. Clearly, the deceptive practice will take hold, as salespeople unburdened by morals are promoted and compensated better than the high-roaders. It's a clear form of Gresham's Law.[25]

In the real estate business, we have brokers who focus on client acquisition and brokers who focus on conveying real property. And if we merge King and Munger, we arrive at: Two distinct competing standards of service, competence, and integrity. Let's call them a low integrity standard and a high integrity standard.

---

[24] I have seen this in several places but they all seem to trace back to Munger. The irony of course is that Berkshire has become one of the largest real estate brokers in the United States and as such benefits from this industry dynamic. I like to think that if Messrs. Buffett and Munger would spend an hour with a typical real estate coach and their broker clientele, they would promptly exit the business. Not only are these gentlemen Captains of Industry, but both have written extensively on business ethics. I just find it impossible to believe that Buffett and Munger would find the ethical standards of this business acceptable. But as of this writing, Buffett is 89 and Munger is 96. So I'm not sure they'll get around to this.

[25] See: *Gresham's Law: Why Bad Drives Out Good As Time Passes*, Farnam Street Blog, December 2009. Find it here: https://fs.blog/2009/12/mental-model-greshams-law/

And we have consumers with imperfect information, limited experience, and inadequate knowledge and understanding of the market. Over the course of a lifetime, most consumers only enter the real estate marketplace occasionally. So some will unknowingly accept the lesser standard. Others will accept it based on pretense and stereotype and sometimes just sheer credulousness. And if the price is right, others will not care about these standards one way or the other.

Finally there is no real penalty to brokers for maintaining a low integrity standard. They are not penalized by the market or by industry norms or ethical requirements. In fact, the only real consequence is when and if they choose the high integrity standard: They make less money.

So combine these three factors: Consumers with imperfect information, brokers with two distinct competing standards of integrity, and little or no consequence for the low integrity standard, and you have the perfect environment for Gresham's Law to take root.

It is not that brokers actually choose the low integrity standard. But they do choose to focus their attention on client acquisition above all else. Client acquisition becomes the singular focus and with little downside. And competence at conveying real property takes time and effort. This is the actual choice brokers make: A focus on client acquisition or a focus on conveying real property. And hopefully over the course of this book, I have convinced you that this truly is a choice.

In the real estate business we reward low integrity, and just as importantly, we fail to reward high integrity. And this goes largely unnoticed by our customers, and therefore, unpenalized. To use the Farnam Street language, the low integrity brokers gain a sustainable competitive advantage over the high integrity brokers. *Client acquisition* gains a sustainable competitive advantage over *conveying real property.*

The bad drives out the good. The unworthy drives out the worthy. The lesser standard drives out the higher standard. Bad service drives out good service. Bad morals drive out good morals. Incompetence drives out competence. The low integrity brokers drive out the high integrity brokers.

Before we leave, is it either/or? That is, surely there are brokers who focus just enough on client acquisition so that they can spend an adequate amount of time on conveying real property? And vice versa. And the answer is: Yes, there are *some*. But they don't call it Gresham's *Law* for nothing. As Mackenzie King pointed out, the incentives favor the inferior standard, and over time this is what prevails. Sadly, this is what we see in the real estate business.

Now, this is a rather bleak assessment of the business. Must it be so? And is it static? If I thought *yes* was the answer to either question, I would not have bothered writing this book. This work is my attempt to shine a light on the problem. I hope that broader understanding of the problem, by consumers and brokers, puts us on the path to resolution; the path to competence and integrity. Only together can we change the low integrity industry dynamic. Demand better.

And with technology advances, more of the real estate process will be turned over to the consumers themselves. Hopefully this will lift some of the murkiness, and consumers will notice the nonsense and understand that they should not tolerate it. One hopes.

Afterword: Competence and Integrity

Now some will read this book and say: *Man, you really just don't like real estate brokers, do you?* Well it's true, I don't have much use for brokers who focus on *client acquisition*:

- Brokers who pretend that real estate is a sales job
- Brokers who use scripts and hire coaches
- Brokers who practice dual agency
- Brokers who hawk coming soon to advance dual agency
- Brokers who do not respect their clients and potential clients
- Brokers who are not honest with their clients or who spout malarkey because they are afraid to be truthful.
- Brokers who fail to offer their clients objectivity
- Brokers who are aggressive and pushy, stupid and lazy
- Brokers who underprice properties
- Brokers who care more about a quick and easy paycheck rather than the best interests of their clients
- Brokers who lack technical skills or business savvy
- Brokers with dysfunctional or illusory teams
- Brokers who sound authoritative but really don't know what they are talking about
- Brokers who are inflexible regarding fees
- Brokers who offer the illusion of high service
- Brokers who refuse to compete on their actual value proposition
- Brokers who exploit fear and nervousness
- Brokers who attempt to shift their duties to the other side
- Brokers who are less than forthright regarding the goals of marketing and open houses
- Brokers who never take the time to fully understand their state's offer and contract, and how to use it to serve their clients
- Brokers who view real negotiation skill as unimportant

I could go on, but notice one thing about this list: These are all choices that brokers make. And this list is before we get to brokers who lie and brokers who steal. Which are also choices. We have not discussed misrepresentation or misappropriation. I may not approve of the brokers who focus on *client acquisition*, but their activities and shenanigans are legal. So while this may not be a question of legality, it is a question of integrity. And the acceptability of low integrity choices, which become standard. Enter Gresham's Law for Real Estate.

Now, you may justifiably ask: *Well, who's left? Surely the above list must include just about everyone in the business.* But it does not; not by far. Because these attributes tend to overlap. If you see one, I would urge you to look for others. Start with dual agency, because it is a simple question to ask, and then keep your eyes open.

Competence is a choice. And a character trait. It is a function of integrity. That is how I started this book.

If we accept that competence is a choice, how could we possibly believe otherwise? Can one have integrity and yet *not* choose competence? No, in the business of real estate brokerage, if you want to claim integrity, you must first work on your competence. You must choose to be competent. And that competence must be purposefully acquired.

What is the alternative? No one chooses to be incompetent. But brokers certainly do choose to focus their attention elsewhere, and thereby neglect or ignore transactional competence. That is a choice they make.

And making this choice, the brokers demonstrate a complete lack of regard and respect for their clients. I can think of no other business where so many of the so-called professionals hold their customers and clients in such low regard. Surely this, too, is a question of integrity.

I hope you found this entire book to be about integrity. Because competence in the real estate business is really about integrity in the real estate business. Of course, all brokers proclaim competence and integrity. So it is my sincere hope that this book has helped you, broker and consumer alike, determine what these qualities look like and how to find them.

Now please, insist on them.

Reuben Moore
Cary, North Carolina
September, 2020

Glossary

A real estate glossary like no other.

assessment or **special assessment** Fee or charge imposed by a *homeowners' association (HOA)* in excess of funds raised by the monthly fees, usually a one-time expense for a major repair or improvement. Assessment can also refer to a similar charge by a public authority to pay the cost of public improvements. And to the process of determining real property value for property taxes.

best practices Commercial or professional procedures that are accepted or prescribed as being correct or most effective (Oxford English Dictionary). I personally believe that best practices also encompass high competence and high integrity practices, along with high ethical standards.

breach The breaking of a law, or failure of duty, either by omission or commission; the failure to perform, without legal excuse, any promise that forms a part or the whole of a contract (North Carolina Real Estate Commission).

business model A plan for the successful operation of a business, typically identifying sources of revenue, intended customer base, products, and details of financing (Oxford English Dictionary). In residential real estate brokerage we are seeing a proliferation of various and new models. In addition to the traditional model, we have discount brokerage with *flat-fees*, limited-service, *entry-only*, *commission rebates*, etc. *iBuyers* offer a new and interesting business model. I hope we will soon see fee-for-service and hourly-billing models. The online system for buyers and sellers I describe in Chapter 30 offers yet another possible business model.

buying the listing The argument that seducing sellers with an inflated and unrealistic price is dishonest because brokers fully intend to lower the price in order to get the property sold. Often used as a justification for underpricing.

client acquisition The broker skill set necessary to acquire clients. To be successful in the real estate business, it is vital to have, or to generate, a stream of potential clients. This is so important that brokers will concentrate their time, effort, and money, on this aspect of the business to the detriment of all others. Client acquisition is a sales pursuit. Also used to describe brokers who focus on this skill set. See *rhinestone cowboy*.

coach or **real estate coach** A class of consultant that brokers hire to help the broker acquire and manipulate clients. Essentially sales coaches. Primarily responsible for the *scripts* used in the business.

coming soon An attempt by a broker to lead a seller into a *single-agent dual agency* situation by limiting other brokers' access to the property, and thereby also securing the buyer as a client.

commission rebate A form of discount buyer agency where the buyer's broker will pay (or rebate) some portion of his commission to the buyer. This money technically moves from the seller to the listing broker to the buyer's broker to the buyer. And clearly the buyer's broker can do as he pleases with his money, including give some of it to the buyer. But arguably this is tantamount to an involuntary money transfer from the seller to the buyer as an inducement to buy the property.

commodity A raw material, primary product, or other basic good which is traded in bulk and the units of which are interchangeable for the purposes of trading. In contemporary use, non-tangible resources such as electricity or internet bandwidth, or services such as freight or insurance, are often classed (and traded) as commodities, especially when they are fungible or interchangeable (Oxford English Dictionary). Wikipedia offers a more concise version: In economics, a commodity is an economic good or service that has full or substantial fungibility: That is, the market treats instances of the good or service as equivalent, or nearly so, with no regard to who produced them. Competently executed basic residential property marketing is entirely fungible, and therefore a commodity service.

comparable or **comp** A recently sold property that has similar characteristics to a property being appraised or otherwise valued (the subject property) and that is used for comparative purposes when estimating the value of the subject property (North Carolina Real Estate Commission).

comparable market analysis (CMA) A study of recent sales of comparable properties used by real estate brokers to estimate the market value of property for a buyer or seller in connection with a real estate transaction (North Carolina Real Estate Commission). In the year 2020, I see absolutely no reason why this process could not be automated in such a way to produce viable and accurate results for most residential properties.

conveying real property The broker skill set necessary for transactional competence. The customer service aspect of the real estate business. Conveying real property is not a sales pursuit. Also used to describe brokers who focus on this skill set. See *George Bailey*.

copy The text of an advertisement or other marketing asset.

counterpart A person or thing that corresponds to or has the same function as another person or thing in a different place or situation (Oxford Free Dictionary Online). I use this term when discussing *the other side*. Jim Camp prefers the term *respected adversary*. In any case, the parties on the other side are not your friends. And even if they are friends, for the purposes of a real estate negotiation and transaction, one should treat them with a certain degree of dispassion.

designated agency A situation where two brokers work for the same firm, but each represents one of the parties in a particular transaction.

disclosure statement or **property disclosure statement** A seller-initiated form used to disclose material facts to a buyer or a potential buyer.

dual agency A situation where one firm represents *both* the buyer and the seller in a single transaction. In these situations, it is helpful to make a distinction between *designated agency* and *single-agent dual agency*.

due diligence The contractual concept that a buyer will be given an option to purchase property for some period of time, the *Due Diligence Period*. Also refers to a buyer's investigation of the property during this period.

Due Diligence Fee The fee the buyer pays the seller for the option to purchase during the *Due Diligence Period*. This fee is nonrefundable. If during this period, the buyer decides to terminate the contract (typically for any reason or no reason), the seller keeps the fee. And if the buyer does not terminate and therefore moves forward with the transaction, the fee is applied to the *Purchase Price*.

Due Diligence Period The time period a buyer is given for making the decision whether to move forward with a purchase or to terminate the contract.

duty shifting Any attempt by a real estate broker to shift one or more of *their duties to their own client* to the broker on the other side.

easement A right to use land owned by another person or entity for a special purpose, such as a right-of-way to go across the property.

entry-only A form of discount listing where the listing broker will enter the property into the Multiple Listing Service (MLS) only. The broker provides no additional services.

feedback (buyer) Notes that a buyer's broker will share with the listing broker and seller after viewing a property.

fiduciary The North Carolina Real Estate Commission offers a nice definition: A relationship wherein one party imposes special trust and confidence in another party, usually involving the holding or managing of money or other property. An example is the relationship between a real estate broker and his principal. Also refers to the party in whom the special trust and confidence is placed. So, one who acts on behalf of another, putting that person's interests first and certainly ahead of their own.

flat-fee A brokerage fee arrangement that involves the payment of a fixed fee to a broker. The fee is not a percentage of the ultimate sales price, and may not even be tied to a given transaction's consummation.

George Bailey A quietly competent real estate practitioner, not afraid of hard work or getting his hands dirty; never a hotshot, but consistently reliable, levelheaded, and scrupulously honest. Perhaps sometimes undervalued or underestimated. I use this term to represent brokers who focus on *conveying real property*.

Gresham's Law Originally, *bad money drives out good*. Later: If we make no distinction for the worthy and no penalty for the unworthy, the unworthy proliferates, and over time becomes the new standard. Finally, the Charlie Munger definition: Bad morals drive out the good; unethical behavior is contagious.

Gresham's Law for Real Estate The incompetent, low integrity brokers drive out the competent, high integrity brokers. Those brokers who focus on *client acquisition* drive out the brokers who focus on *conveying real property*.

gunslinger An aggressive and competent hotshot real estate practitioner.

homeowners' association (HOA) An organization charged with maintaining common areas and shared structures and amenities of a subdivision or condominium or townhouse development. Also charged with insuring adherence to the association's covenants, restrictions, and rules. Sometimes referred to as a *property owners' association* (POA).

iBuyer A firm that purchases off-market properties for less than fair market value by offering the sellers convenience and expedience. They make money by charging the sellers a fee and also by selling the properties at or above fair market value.

malarkey Something that a real estate broker will say, often in response to a question, in order to avoid saying *I'm not sure* or *I don't know*. The broker fears that these truthful responses will make him look unknowledgeable or even incompetent.

malfeasance Wrongdoing or misconduct, especially by a public official. In addition to public officials, we can extend this term to anyone in a position of responsibility and certainly to fiduciaries. For instance, we read about corporate malfeasance. I use as a generic term for wrongdoing or misconduct, especially of a business or financial nature. Note the OED's second definition is simply: *Wrongdoing*.

material fact Fact about a property or a buyer which must be disclosed to the other side (by a broker, but not necessarily by the seller or buyer themselves).

misappropriation Appropriation of something for wrong use; especially the action or an instance of taking (funds, etc.) fraudulently or unfairly (Oxford English Dictionary). I think a simpler definition is: Appropriation by theft or embezzlement.

misrepresentation A false representation, either willful or negligent or fraudulent, of a *material fact* to another party (North Carolina Real Estate Commission).

Multiple Listing Service (MLS) The formerly print and now online database of all available properties listed by member brokers, and maintained by the local REALTOR® association. Includes currently available properties and a history of transactions and activity.

negotiation I like Jim Camp's definition best: An agreement between two or more parties, with all parties having the right to veto.

objections Label brokers give to anything that clients or potential clients do not want to do. Objections must be *handled* or *overcome*, often using *scripts*.

odd pricing Pricing that does not end in a zero or a number of zeros. For instance, $1.99. Conventional wisdom and numerous studies say it works because people read left to right. Therefore, the left-most figure is the most important in terms of perception.

omission The willful or negligent failure to disclose a *material fact* to another party (North Carolina Real Estate Commission).

pain or **cause pain** In a real estate negotiation and transaction, a financial loss that the counterparts are unable to endure or are unwilling to accept. Or perhaps ultimately do accept, but only after all else fails. Pain is a harsh word, and may even be offensive to some who perhaps feel it turns negotiation and business into a blood sport. I appreciate this concern, but use pain only as a technical and financial term.

REALTOR® A member of the National Association of REALTORS®, a trade organization of real estate brokers. Not all brokers belong to this group. The primary requirement for becoming a REALTOR® is agreeing to abide by the *REALTOR® Code of Ethics*.

REALTOR® Code of Ethics The REALTOR® codification of ethical duties. It consists of seventeen articles describing REALTOR® duties to clients and customers, to the public, and to other REALTORS®.

REALTOR® Code of Ethics, Article 15 Let's quote it here: *REALTORS® shall not knowingly or recklessly make false or misleading statements about other real estate professionals, their businesses, or their business practices.*

rhinestone cowboy A glitzy and inauthentic pretender. I use this term to represent real estate brokers who focus on *client acquisition*, and not on *conveying real property*. See *client acquisition*.

script-reader A broker who uses scripts.

scripted exchange A fake conversation where a broker uses scripts in an attempt to control and manipulate the other party or parties to the *conversation*.

scripts Canned responses that brokers use to control and manipulate *conversations*.

signaling Economic concept where firms and individuals signal their competence and value through pricing, credentials, appearance, presentation, location, and other attributes.

single-agent dual agency A situation where one individual broker supposedly represents *both* the buyer and the seller in a single transaction, and therefore makes more money, often double.

sunk cost In economics and finance, a cost that has already been incurred and that cannot be recovered. In economic decision making, sunk costs are treated as bygone and are not taken into consideration when deciding whether to continue an investment project (Encyclopædia Britannica).

survey The process of determining the quantity and boundaries of a parcel of real estate. Also, the report and diagram of such findings.

syndication The process of a local Multiple Listing Service (MLS) transmitting listing data to other online sites. These other sites include large players like Zillow, but also the websites of other broker members of the MLS. The result is that essentially all online sites include most if not all active properties. Essentially all sites are receiving the same data from the same data feed.

value At its simplest level, value is *service* over *price*. Therefore, neither service nor price, alone, determine value.

value proposition The service-level and price combination that an individual or firm offers consumers in a given market.

win-win Let's use the Harvard Program on Negotiation definition: Win-win negotiations are those negotiations in which each party walks away from the bargaining table having achieved its goals within the confines of an integrative, or value-creating, bargaining process. Win-win strategies are all about increasing your opponent's satisfaction even as you achieve the outcome you desire.

zebra (solid brown) Metaphor used to demonstrate the concept that people hire their *idea of a broker*, good or bad, regardless of that broker's competence or integrity. If someone does not meet the stereotype or look the part, he or she does not get hired for the role.

zero-sum game A situation in which a gain for one side entails a corresponding loss by the other side, such that the net change is always zero.

Acknowledgements

Thanks to Mira who makes everything possible.

Special thanks to my long time colleagues in the real estate business including Vanna Langdon, Mike Bower, Ed Gobble, and Susan Hustace, all of whom have taught me so much.

Thanks to Kevin Stewman and Chad & Leslie Shoaf for being straight shooters in a murky business.

Thanks to Gary Sutton, Steve Smallman, David Barrier, Andy Holloman, and Chris Adams for years of wisdom.

Thanks also to Sherry Shaw for invaluable writing and editing advice.

I would like to thank Richard Armstrong for being an early reader, editor, and advisor. More than anyone, you helped make this work stronger, tighter, and more readable.

I would like to thank my clients who have helped me so much more than I ever helped them. Especially my friends, Walter & Karen High, who were also my first and last clients. Thank you both.

Finally, I would like to thank the readers of this book. I hope you found it useful for your own real estate endeavors. Please help me improve the business by sharing this book with others.

About the author

Reuben Moore has been an actively licensed real estate broker in the Research Triangle Park area of North Carolina since 2003, working on both the residential and commercial sides of the business. He is Managing Broker and Broker-in-Charge of Brick and Garden Real Estate, in Cary, North Carolina. Previously he owned and operated Moore Books and Books Over Franklin in Chapel Hill. A North Carolina native, he graduated from the University of North Carolina at Chapel Hill with a BSBA in finance.

You can reach him at: ReubenMoore@iCloud.com

Moore's Real Estate Review

Our discussion continues at:
https://MooresRealEstate.blogspot.com

Volume Purchase Discounts

Interested in purchasing ten or more copies of this book? Email the author for a *Discount Schedule*. Please note: We can only offer volume discounts for the paperback version of the book.

www.ingramcontent.com/pod-product-compliance
Lightning Source LLC
Chambersburg PA
CBHW071353210526
45465CB00001B/75